GUEST EDITORS' NOTE

CONTEXT FOR OUR WORK ON ACHIEVEMENT-LEVEL SETTING

In 1990, the National Assessment Governing Board (NAGB) began its groundbreaking work on the development of performance standards for student achievement. As policymakers for the National Assessment of Educational Progress (NAEP), they sought not only to describe what American students know and can do in core subject areas but also to define what students should know and be able to accomplish. In keeping with a historic commitment to reporting NAEP results on metrics understandable to policymakers and the public, the Board has developed performance standards to chart the United States' progress toward high academic attainment.

In the 1970s and early 1980s, NAEP reports were built around the assessment materials themselves; by displaying assessment items and associated student performance data, initial reports allowed NAEP users to review the types of tasks students could and could not do. In NAEP's second generation, item response data were summarized across tasks to provide a picture of overall performance for NAEP test takers. Group performance was reported generally on a 500-point scale, along with descriptions of the knowledge and skills typical of performance at given scaled scores. Current reports continue this convention.

NAGB's recent work on performance standards for NAEP adds fundamentally new data to NAEP reporting. The Board has developed guidelines and a process for setting performance standards that indicate "how good is good enough" in reading, math, history, geography, science, and the other NAEP subject areas. This is done by establishing a priori policy definitions for three performance levels, applying them to specific content domains and test results, and then reporting numbers of students performing at basic, proficient, and advanced achievement levels. The NAEP performance levels stay fixed for multiple administrations in a subject area, providing a mechanism to observe changes in these percentages over time and, in this way, bring NAEP even closer to an understandable, policy-relevant reporting metric.

Requests for reprints should be sent to James Pellegrino, Peabody College of Education and Human Development, Vanderbilt University, P.O. Box 329, Nashville, TN 37203. E-mail: pellegjw@ctrvax.vanderbilt.edu

PRIOR EVALUATORS' ASSESSMENTS

Despite the important goals of this work, NAEP's standards have been criticized by the National Academy of Education (NAE, 1996), the General Accounting Office (1993), and others. NAEP's standards are derived using the most prevalent standard-setting model currently in use. With the Angoff approach and its variants, panels of experts are convened, trained on the knowledge and skills of examinees who meet minimum criteria for inclusion at a given performance level, and then asked to make judgments about the probable performance of these examinees on individual test items. Although the Angoff method has provided plausible results in other settings, some believe that item-by-item methods for setting performance standards are fundamentally flawed when applied to student assessments like NAEP. In the NAEP context, raters are asked to estimate the probability that a hypothetical student at the boundary of a given achievement level will get an item correct. This requires judges to delineate the ways students could answer an item, relate these to cognitive processes that students may or may not possess, and operationally link these processes with the categorization of performance at three different levels. Some have argued that this judgment process represents a nearly impossible cognitive task (NAE, 1996).

Further, evaluators have pointed to internal inconsistencies in the ratings generated for different types of items and the lack of correspondence with other external evidence of student achievement. On past NAEP assessments, for example, notable differences were observed in the cutscores set for each achievement level using right–wrong and extended-response items. Method variance of this kind is problematic because it renders cutscore locations dependent on the mix of item types in the assessment and in the standard setters' ratings, in addition to rendering questionable the verbal description of the meaning of achievement at a given level. The second concern—about inconsistencies with external data—is discussed by the NAE panel (1996) and described in Robert Linn's article in this issue. This criticism concerns inconsistencies between NAEP achievement-level results and data from other assessment programs, including the Advanced Placement tests and Scholastic Aptitude Test, where larger proportions of students perform at high levels than are indicated by NAEP standards.

OUR CONTRIBUTION TO THE DEBATE

Despite the criticisms, there are no widely accepted alternate methods for setting standards for student achievement. The NAE and others have urged NAEP's stewards to investigate alternate models for standard setting. NAGB and the National Center for Education Statistics (NCES) have looked to the academic community for guidance in identifying and adapting other models. To this end,

NAGB and NCES sponsored a standard-setting conference in 1994, but conference organizers concluded that much remains to be learned about standard setting for large-scale assessments.

Congress has asked the National Academy of Sciences' (NAS) Committee on the Evaluation of NAEP to review NAEP generally and evaluate the state assessments, student performance levels, and the extent to which NAEP provides results that are reasonable, valid, and informative to the public. This special issue includes a series of articles that inform our work on standard setting. To explore standard-setting models from other fields and to determine if they suggest alternate paradigms for defining future NAEP performance levels, we sponsored a workshop on standard setting in December 1996.

We began our workshop with a description and examination of the current NAEP standard-setting model, then looked to standard-setting applications outside of education. These applications included those that focus on human performance and the adequacy of human performance; in these contexts, raters were asked to focus on the knowledge and skills that underlie competent performance. We also examined applications that focus on the impact of environmental agents on life and the ecology; in these cases, raters began with the knowledge that more (or less) of a substance is better and, as for NAEP, the judgment task is to determine "how good is good enough." We wished to examine parallels in the objectives, empirical grounding, judgmental requirements, and policy tensions for standard setting in NAEP and in other domains.

FORMAT OF THIS ISSUE

The structure of this issue follows that of the workshop. The first three articles focus on standard setting in the context of NAEP. The first article in this issue, by Mark Reckase, describes the process currently used to build consensus about the knowledge and skills students should exhibit on NAEP and the levels at which students should demonstrate what they know and can do. The most recent NAEP science assessment is used as the illustrative case. The second article, by Robert Linn, discusses how the validity of NAEP achievement levels may be defined, illustrates three potential validity problems with the current NAEP achievement levels, and discusses research designs for validating inferences from NAEP achievement-level results. The third article, by Robert Mislevy, suggests revisions to standard setting and reporting that may accompany recently debated revisions to NAEP for the year 2000. Specifically, Robert Mislevy talks about the implications of using a fixed, representative subset (i.e., a market basket) of items in contrast to the current matrix-sampling construction. In considering this alternative approach, he provides a larger framework that helps explicate the overall inferential scheme in which current and future NAEP reporting occurs.

The next four authors describe standard-setting efforts outside education. The first two describe standard-setting applications for which judgments are made about human knowledge, skills, and performance. Barbara Plake discusses applications in licensure and certification derived from surveying a variety of fields of endeavor. She focuses on the types of tasks used to assess performance and the related methods for then setting standards. Lawrence Hanser describes several areas of military personnel and performance standards and how they are determined. The last two articles present information about standards for environmental agents. Jeanne Goldberg presents information about the data and values that underlie nutritional guidelines, and Sheila Jasanoff discusses standard-setting models and applications in environmental regulation.

TENSIONS, CONSEQUENCES, AND PRAGMATISM

We commissioned these articles to examine the current state of affairs and residual issues with respect to achievement-level setting in NAEP and to help us determine whether the models and methods used in other disciplines have useful application to education. It is important to note that the articles represent the authors' views, not necessarily those of the committee or National Research Council. The articles in this issue and our workshop discussion point out a number of analogies between the objectives, requisite data, judgment requirements and policy issues for NAEP and other applications; several of the parallels are discussed later.

Tensions

First, the articles on standard setting in alternative contexts suggest that the tensions that surround the combination of science and judgment in standard setting are not unique to achievement-level setting in NAEP. Experts in licensure and certification, in the military, in nutrition, and in environmental regulation all balance incomplete and inadequate data with value judgments about desired outcomes. In setting environmental standards, for example, the efficacy and economic costs of meeting alternative standards must be weighed against their impact on citizens most at risk.

Consequences

Second, some of the authors describe applications for which standard setters and their audiences can gauge the consequences of performance at given levels. This is particularly apparent in the military context where the ability to talk about the consequences of entry-level or training standards on soldier performance simplifies the development of standards and reporting of results in important ways. In contrast, NAEP standard setters and standards users are hampered by an inability to talk about the consequences of data showing large (or small) proportions of individuals performing at high levels.

Robert Linn argues in his article that in cases where it is difficult to explicitly state the likely outcomes of performance at different levels, it may be sufficient to establish cutpoints at substantively important points on the scale, to fix those cutpoints, and then to examine performance changes over time. Observing that over time more (or fewer) students demonstrate the knowledge and skills associated with a particular cutpoint, he suggests, is meaningful and potentially useful information.

Pragmatism

Finally, the authors suggest that pragmatism must guide standard setting. It probably does not make sense to define performance levels that far exceed observed performance. In the recent past, and for multiple subject areas and grades, fewer than 5% of students purportedly performed at advanced levels on NAEP and less than 30% scored at proficient. The data would hold more meaning for policymakers and the public and their implications would be clearer if the standards were not so far ahead of observed performance. And, as earlier noted, the data are hard to reconcile with other indicators of educational performance.

As editors of this issue, we posit that sparse evidence of the use of achievement-level results by education policymakers may, in part, be a function of the very high standards that have been set and the very low proportions of students performing at or above the proficient levels. It also may be attributable to the conceptual difficulty of juxtaposing information about what students "know and can do" with achievement levels whose meaning reflects policy positions regarding what they "should know and be able to do." This can be a daunting distinction for any person to fully comprehend and, thus, may impact the utility of these results.

POSTSCRIPT

The NAS Committee on the Evaluation of NAEP continues to evaluate the achievement-level setting process and alternate paradigms for setting NAEP performance levels. Of additional interest are conceptual issues such as the meaning of achievement levels and their linkage to the entire NAEP design, starting with content frameworks and extending through item and test development, test scoring, and reporting of results. We hope that this issue and wide distribution of these articles will prompt others to join in this interesting analysis and debate.

REFERENCES

General Accounting Office. (1993). *Educational achievement standards: NAGB's approach yields misleading interpretations.* Washington, DC: Author.

National Academy of Education. (1996). *Quality and utility: The 1994 trial state assessment in reading.* Stanford, CA: Author.

> James Pellegrino, Chair
> Lauress Wise and Nambury Raju, Members
> National Academy of Sciences' Committee on the Evaluation
>   of National and State Assessments of Educational Progress
> *Guest Editors*

NATIONAL ACADEMY OF SCIENCES' COMMITTEE ON THE EVALUATION OF THE NATIONAL AND STATE ASSESSMENTS OF EDUCATIONAL PROGRESS

James W. Pellegrino (Chair), *Peabody College of Education and Human Development and Learning Technology Center, Vanderbilt University, Nashville, TN*
Gail Baxter, *School of Education, University of Michigan, Ann Arbor*
Norman M. Bradburn, *National Opinion Research Center, University of Chicago, IL*
Thomas P. Carpenter, *Wisconsin Center for Educational Research, University of Wisconsin, Madison*
Allan Collins, *Bolt, Beranek and Newman, Inc., Cambridge, MA*
Stephen B. Dunbar, *College of Education, University of Iowa, Iowa City*
Larry V. Hedges, *Department of Education, University of Chicago, IL*
Sharon Johnson-Lewis, *The Council of Great City Schools, Washington, DC*
Roderick J. A. Little, *Department of Biostatistics, University of Michigan, Ann Arbor*
Elsie G. J. Moore, *College of Education, Arizona State University, Tempe*
Nambury S. Raju, *Institute of Psychology, Illinois Institute of Technology, Chicago*
Marlene Scardamalia, *Centre for Applied Cognitive Science, Ontario Institute for Studies in Education, Toronto, Canada*
Guadalupe Valdés, *School of Education and Department of Spanish and Portuguese, Stanford University, CA*
Sheila W. Valencia, *College of Education, University of Washington, Seattle*
Lauress L. Wise, *Human Resources Research Organization, Alexandria, VA*

Converting Boundaries Between National Assessment Governing Board Performance Categories to Points on the National Assessment of Educational Progress Score Scale: The 1996 Science NAEP Process

Mark D. Reckase
ACT, Inc.
Iowa City, Iowa

National Assessment Governing Board (NAGB) policy indicates that results from the National Assessment of Educational Progress (NAEP) should be reported according to the percentage of students estimated to be above 3 levels of standards called achievement levels. The standards, labeled Basic, Proficient, and Advanced, are operationalized by 3 points on the NAEP scale. In this article, I provide an overview of the process that was used to identify provisional locations for the points that would inform NAGB as they set the achievement levels for the science NAEP. The process includes the identification of panelists to be involved in the achievement-level setting, the training for the panelists, and the method for converting panelists ratings of NAEP items to points on the NAEP score scale.

In September 1993, American College Testing (ACT) undertook work under contract to the National Assessment Governing Board (NAGB) to design and implement a process for recommending to NAGB numeric points on the National Assessment of Educational Progress (NAEP) score scales for U.S. history, world geography, and science that correspond to the boundaries between performance

---

Requests for reprints should be sent to Mark D. Reckase, ACT, Inc., P.O. Box 168, Iowa City, IA 52243.

TABLE 1
Constraints on the Process for Translating the Policy Definitions to Regions on the NAEP Reporting Scale

1. The process should be completed by using the judgments of a carefully selected panel of teachers (55%), nonteacher educators (15%), and members of the general public (30%).
2. The translation from the policy definitions to the NAEP reporting scale should be done in the context of the content framework that serves as the basis for the assessment.
3. The translation process must be consistent with the matrix sampling procedures used to collect the assessment data and with the IRT–plausible-values methodology used to create the NAEP reporting scale.
4. The translation process must work with the complex structure of the assessment, including the subscales, the weights for combining the subscales into an overall score, and the wide variety of types of assessment tasks.

Note. NAEP = National Assessment of Educational Progress; IRT = item response theory.

categories defined by NAGB policy. The three performance categories (NAGB, 1995), or achievement levels, are defined as follows:

1. *Proficient* represents solid academic performance for each grade level assessed. Students reaching this level have demonstrated subject matter knowledge, the ability to apply such knowledge to real-world situations, and the analytical skills appropriate to the subject matter.

2. *Basic* denotes partial mastery of prerequisite knowledge and skills that are fundamental for proficient work at each grade.

3. *Advanced* signifies superior performance beyond proficient.

The three definitions, which will be called "policy definitions" to distinguish them from other content-specific performance descriptions, provide the performance standards used for NAEP reporting. It was not ACT's task to produce new standards but to translate only the standards implied by the policy definitions onto the NAEP reporting scale for a particular content area.[1] The process used for translation has become known as the achievement levels setting (ALS) process. The translation process was performed within certain constraints specified in the contract with NAGB and inherent in the NAEP assessment process. These constraints are summarized in Table 1.

As the process for translating the policy definitions into recommended regions on the NAEP reporting scale is described, the impact of the constraints will be emphasized.

---

[1]The National Assessment of Education Progress reporting scale is typically a weighted combination of item response theory-based θ-scales (Allen, Johnson, Mislevy, & Thomas, 1996) with a range from about 50 to 250. The weights for each of the θ-scales are specified in the framework for the test (National Assessment Governing Board, 1996).

SOME BASIC CONCEPTS

The NAEP reporting scale defines a continuum of performance for a content area that ranges from a low scale score of about 50 to a maximum scale score of about 250. The challenge to the ALS process is to map the policy definitions into regions on the NAEP scale. The policy definitions refer to ranges of performance rather than points on the score scale. All students who score higher than the lower boundary of an achievement level are considered to be at or above that level. For example, all students who score higher than the lower boundary of the advanced achievement level are considered to be "advanced."[2] The estimated percentage of the total student population for the grade level who fall at or above each achievement-level boundary is provided in NAEP reports. The "below basic" category is not defined as an achievement level, but it is included in the reports.

To define the score ranges that correspond to the achievement-level categories, three points need to be estimated on the NAEP scale. These points are the lower boundaries of each of the three achievement-level categories. The ALS process that has been developed focuses on judgmentally estimating the skills and knowledge that define the lower bound of each policy definition in terms of content and skills from the frameworks. Those skill definitions are then mapped onto the NAEP reporting scale, using estimates of performance on actual NAEP items.

The entire ALS process has only three major steps: (a) educate panelists about NAGB policy, the framework, and the NAEP test; (b) help the panelists conceptualize the capabilities of the least able student in each achievement-level category (e.g., borderline students); and (c) have the panelists estimate how well the borderline students will perform on NAEP tasks and map the results onto the NAEP reporting scale. Of course, each of these steps is quite complex, as discussed later.

THE PROCESS

The details of the process for estimating the points corresponding to the boundaries between NAGB policy definitions on the NAEP reporting scale will be provided in the context of the 1996 Science NAEP. Using a specific assessment standard will make the process concrete and also provide specific examples of the complexity of the process.

---

[2] In reality, student scores are not reported for Natioanl Assessment of Education Progress (NAEP). Therefore, single students cannot be classified into an achievement level. In theory, if a student took all of the items in the NAEP pool rather than a sample, he or she could be classified into a region with a reasonable level of confidence.

Panelists

The panelists who provide the expertise needed to translate the policy definitions to the NAEP scale must collectively meet the demographic characteristics specified by NAGB policy. They also need to be knowledgeable about the scientific content of the assessment, be familiar with students at the grade level being assessed, and be qualified to represent their demographic group. In addition, ACT recommended to NAGB that the process for selecting the panelists be replicable and that panels be of sufficient size that the standard errors of the achievement-level estimates would be less than .25 on the θ-scale. That is, multiple groups of panelists could be identified, and the outcomes from any one panel would be expected to generalize to other panels. The replicability of the selection process made it possible to identify multiple groups for the purposes of pilot testing various aspects of the process.

To identify groups of individuals who would meet all requirements for the panels, a two-stage process was developed. The first stage consisted of sampling school districts according to a stratified random sampling plan. In each district, persons who were in a position to nominate qualified persons for the panels were identified. For nominators of teachers, these individuals included district superintendents, leaders of teachers' organizations, and state education officials. For the general public participants, nominators included the mayor, the school board president, a person from the chamber of commerce, and management staff at businesses in the community. For nonteacher educators, persons in sampled school districts as well as deans of colleges and universities and science curriculum directors from state departments of education, were used as nominators. All nominators were informed of the qualifications required of the persons they would be nominating. Once the provisional list of panelists was obtained, the candidates were contacted to verify their qualifications and determine their level of interest. The qualifications were reviewed to determine if the candidates had specific training in a relevant area of science and if they had experience with the student age group.

The second stage in the process was to select a set of qualified candidates that matched the demographic requirements for the panels as given in NAGB policy and the ACT Design Document (ACT, 1994). These individuals were invited to participate in the ALS process. If someone declined, a replacement who represented the appropriate demographic categories was selected. The characteristics of the final set of panelists are supplied in Table 2. The process produced a panel that met all of the constraints implied by item 1 in Table 1 and the ACT Design Document.

Training

During the ALS process, panelists were asked to produce three products: (a) revised achievement-level specific content descriptions consistent with the frameworks for

TABLE 2
Science ALS Distribution of Panelists

Type of Panelist	Grade			Total	%
	4	8	12		
Teacher	17	17	17	51	54
Nonteacher	5	6	4	15	16
General public	9	9	10	28	30
Men	15	14	20	49	52
Women	16	18	11	45	48
White	26	27	24	77	82
Minority	5	5	7	17	18

Note. Panelists were distributed by region as follows: West, 24%; Central, 23%; Southeast, 30%; Northeast, 21%; and Territories, 1%. ALS = achievement levels setting.

Grades 4, 8, and 12 that correspond to the policy definitions and the frameworks; (b) estimates of performance on the assessment tasks for students with capabilities at the boundaries of the achievement-level categories for each grade level; and (c) exemplar assessment tasks from the released NAEP pool for use in representing performance at the achievement levels in a tangible way. Producing these products required detailed knowledge of the policy definitions and the NAEP science framework, the NAEP science assessment, the circumstances of administration, and the uses for the NAEP results.

To ensure that all panelists were well versed in the background needed for these tasks, they were sent detailed descriptive information prior to the ALS meeting, and the first step in the ALS process provided them with 1½ days of training on NAEP, NAGB policy, the science framework, the NAEP science assessment, and the judgmental process for estimating performance on the NAEP assessment tasks. This training was designed to familiarize panelists with constraint 2 in Table 1. That is, in modifying the content descriptions, they were not allowed to stray from skills and knowledge contained in the science framework (NAGB, 1996) and how those knowledge and skills related to the NAGB policy definitions.

Achievement-Level Descriptions

After training, the panelists worked to produce a final version of descriptions of what students at each achievement level for Grades 4, 8, and 12 (the grade levels included in the NAEP assessment) know and can produce. Preliminary versions of the descriptions were included in the science framework document (NAGB, 1996, pp. 35–40). The panelists were asked to refine the preliminary descriptions and then focus on the capabilities of students who had the minimum qualifications to be

TABLE 3
Number of Items Rated by Each Panelist by Grade

Grade	Group	Item Type	
		Dichotomous	Polytomous
4	A	36	58
	B	38	57
8	A	47	82
	B	52	78
12	A	46	75
	B	48	72

included in each achievement-level category. Their goal was to come to agreement on descriptors of borderline performance for each achievement level. Approximately 8 hr were allocated for the panelists to discuss and internalize the achievement-level descriptions and the capabilities of borderline students.

The Judgment Process

The panelists were assigned to grade-level groups and then divided into two subgroups that were matched on demographic characteristics. Each subgroup worked with approximately half of the NAEP science pool. The halves of the pool were produced to be as nearly parallel as possible, given the block structure of NAEP. The number of items rated by each group is summarized in Table 3. Although some items were presented to both groups, the majority was not. Thus, two independent estimates of points on the NAEP scale could be obtained from separate groups of individuals estimating performance on separate groups of items. This grouping of panelists and items not only made their assignment more manageable, but also made it possible to estimate the standard error of the point estimates of the achievement-level boundaries.

The process used for estimating performance on the NAEP science tasks differed slightly depending on whether the tasks were scored 0, 1 or on a multipoint rating scale. For the tasks scored 0, 1 (dichotomous items, both multiple choice and open ended), panelists were asked to consider 100 students who were at the boundaries of each achievement-level category and to estimate how many would respond correctly to each of the tasks. They were, in effect, estimating the probability of correct response for each item conditional on the point on the NAEP reporting scale corresponding to their understanding of borderline performance for the achievement level:

$$P(X_i = 1 \mid \theta_{pb}),$$

where x_i is the score on item i, and θ_{pb} is the point on the NAEP scale corresponding to boundary for achievement-level category b as estimated by panelist p.

For assessment tasks scored using a multipoint rating scale (polytomous items), the panelists were asked to estimate the average (mean) score on the task for the 100 borderline students:

$$E(X_i \mid \theta_{pb}),$$

where the symbols are as defined earlier except that x_i can take on the integer values from 1 to n, where n is the number of points on the rating scale used for scoring. Performance estimates for all items were made after panelists took a form of the NAEP science assessment, worked on all of the hands-on tasks for their group, and reviewed actual examples of student work for all extended constructed response items.

Several types of feedback were built into the process so that the panelists could check the reasonableness of their performance estimates. They could then modify their estimates after the feedback. In all, panelists were given three opportunities to provide performance estimates for the NAEP tasks, with feedback after each round of estimates.

After the first round of estimating borderline performance on the NAEP assessment tasks, three types of feedback were provided. First, the estimated locations of the boundaries between the achievement-level categories were presented for the group as a whole as well as for each individual in the group. Figure 1 gives an example of the estimates from the group as a whole, and Figure 2 gives an example of the feedback that includes the point estimates for individual panelists. In Figure 2, each letter represents a different panelist. The letters were codes so that only the individual panelist would know the location of his or her point on the scale. Also, the scale is not the NAEP scale but rather an artificial scale produced by ACT to provide feedback without revealing the final NAEP scale results.

Figure 2 includes the distributions of estimated boundary points for the Proficient and Advanced boundaries for comparison, but focuses on the individual results for the Basic level. Panelists were given two other graphs that showed their individual results for Proficient and Advanced. This feedback allowed panelists to determine whether they were being more or less generous in their estimates of performance than the other panelists. They could also see how widely distributed the boundary points for the different achievement levels were placed.

The second type of feedback was actual test booklets with student responses that correspond to the group-set boundary points. From this feedback, panelists could see the students' work that corresponded to the estimated points on the NAEP scale and determine whether it matched the skills and knowledge in the achievement-level descriptions.

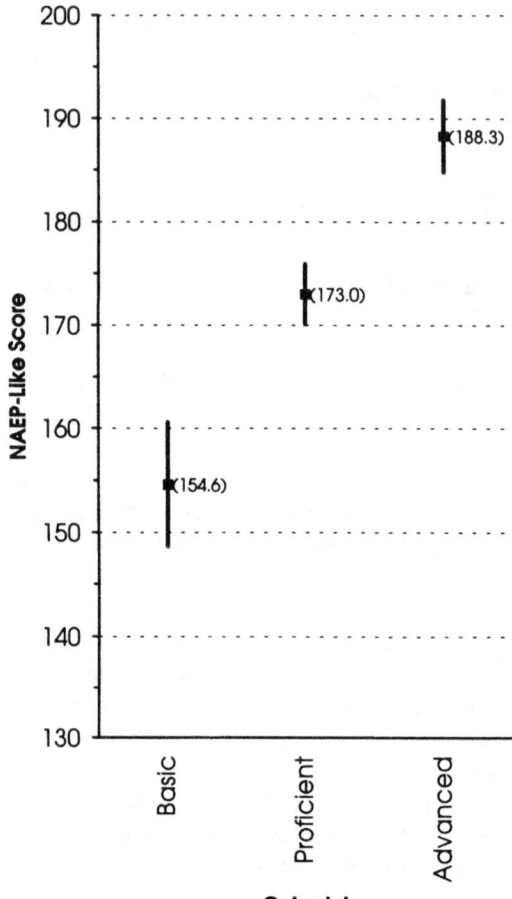

FIGURE 1 Achievement-level boundary estimates and standard deviations on the ACT, Inc. National Assessment of Educational Progress-like scale (science, Grade 12, Round 3).

The third type of feedback was descriptive statistics summarizing actual student performance on the tasks. This feedback included p-values based on all students who took the item for dichotomously scored items, and distributions of performance based on all scoreable responses on the polytomously scored items.

After the feedback, the performance estimates from Round 1 were returned to the panelists, who were then asked to go through the estimation process a second time. They could leave the estimates as the were, or change them in response to the feedback. After Round 2 estimates, the panelists received the same types of feedback as they received after Round 1 but updated to reflect the changes made in their ratings. Thus, panelists could see the consequences of their changes. They were then asked to estimate the borderline performance on the NAEP tasks a third and final time.

Following Round 3, the panelists received the same feedback as before, along with information about the percentage of students who were above each boundary point. They were then asked whether the percentages were reasonable, given their understanding of the policy definitions and the achievement-level descriptions. They could recommend changes in any or all point estimates for their grade.

Mapping to the NAEP Scale

Conceptually, the process for converting the panelists' estimates to the NAEP reporting scale is very straightforward. The estimates for the panelists were converted into average percentage of correct scores and mapped to the NAEP scale using the test characteristics curve (TCC) for the set of items being considered. Figure 3 gives an example of the relation between points on the ACT NAEP-like scale and expected performance on the NAEP item pool. For example, a student with a score of 173 would be expected to get 64.5% of the total points if he or she took the entire item pool. The mapping process uses the TCC to obtain point estimates on the scale, using the relation in the opposite direction. For example, if the panelists judged the percentage of correct score to be 82.1, then the estimated point on the ACT NAEP-like scale would be 188.3.

The process requires three critical assumptions—the same critical assumptions required for estimation of performance for the NAEP examinee sample. These assumptions are not placing more stringent requirements on the ALS process than

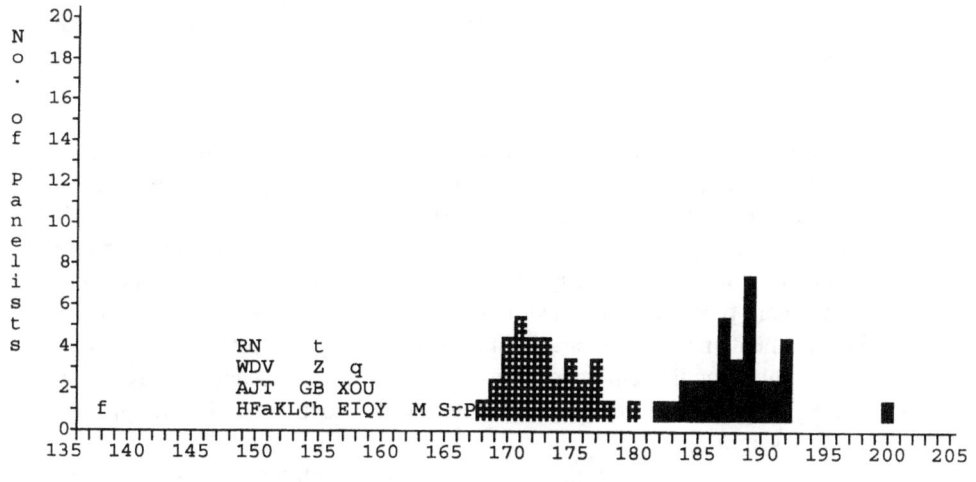

FIGURE 2 Individual feedback; each letter denotes a panelist's estimate.

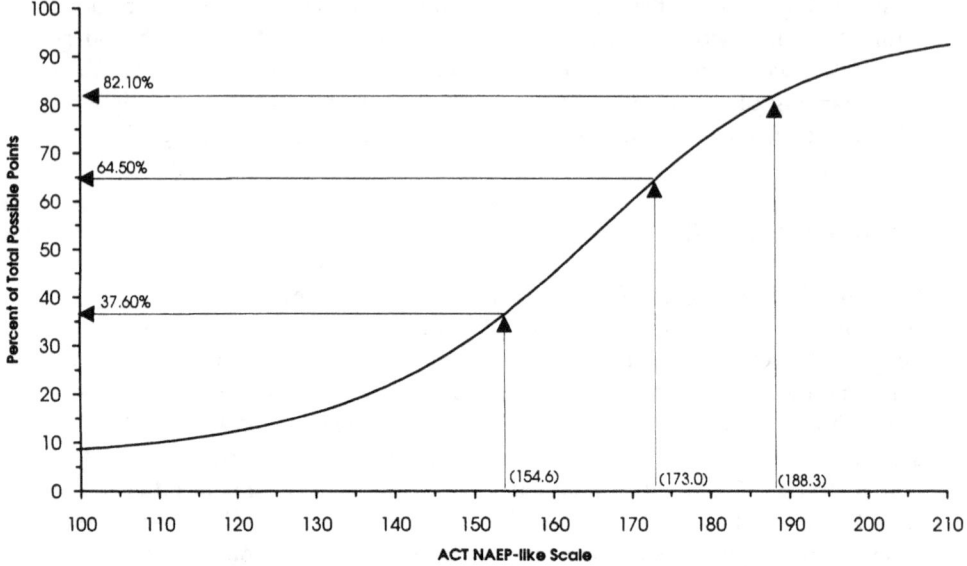

FIGURE 3 Test characteristic curve for Grade 12 item pool.

they do on the NAEP assessment in general. These assumptions are (a) the item characteristic curves (ICCs) for the NAEP tasks are known or at least very well estimated, (b) local independence holds so that it is appropriate to estimate performance on individual tasks and combine these estimates to get an overall estimate, and (c) the scales are reasonably unidimensional. These assumptions are part of constraint 4 in Table 1.

Although this process is conceptually simple, in practice it is very complex. First because there are three different unidimensional scales within the NAEP science assessment, the mapping must be done separately by scale. Second, dichotomous and polytomous items use different item response theory models: the two- and three-parameter logistic (Lord, 1980) and the generalized partial credit model (Muraki, 1992), respectively. In the estimation of student performance, these item types are combined in a way that is weighted by the information provided by the items. Performance estimates were mapped separately for dichotomous and polytomous items and then combined, using a weighted averaging procedure. Information at the point estimate for the group for each item type was used as the weight.

Finally, there were two rating groups of panelists within each grade level that gave estimates on unique sets of items. The results from these rating groups were averaged to get the final estimates of the points on the NAEP scale that define the achievement levels. The following is a step-by-step listing of this mapping process:

1. Average the estimated percentages of correct over panelists and items for each rating group for each scale for the dichotomous items.
2. Map the estimates to the appropriate NAEP subscale for each rating group, using the TCC for each set of dichotomous items used on each scale by each rating group.
3. Average the estimated mean performance over panelists and items for each rating group for each scale for the polytomous items and convert to a percentage-of-maximum-possible score.
4. Map the estimates to the appropriate NAEP subscale for each rating group, using the TCC for each scale for each set of polytomous items used on each scale by each rating group.
5. Combine the polytomous and dichotomous estimates for each subscale by weighing the estimates by the sum of the item information at the estimated boundary point for each item type and dividing by the total information.
6. Combine the estimates on each scale for each rating group, using the scale weights specified in the framework document. This results in point estimates on the final NAEP scale for each rating group.
7. Average the boundary estimates from the two rating groups to get the final point estimates for the boundaries between the achievement levels.

This complex mapping process is necessary because of constraints 3 and 4 in Table 1.[3]

The standard error of the final estimates is given by the difference between the estimates for the two rating groups divided by 2.0. This standard error includes error due to rating group differences and differences in the sets of items used by the two rating groups. To some extent, error in the estimation of the ICCs is also included. The standard error estimate does not include differences in estimates over time or differences in implementation of the process by different facilitators. Certainly, the method of standard error estimation does not consider differences in standard setting methodology. In general, the standard error estimates were acceptably small (from 2.6–10.1 on the ACT NAEP-like scale), indicating that the subgroups generated similar point estimates and that the error due to selection of items and estimation of the ICCs was fairly small.

PANELISTS' REACTION TO THE PROCESS

After each step in the process, the panelists were asked to fill out questionnaires that asked for information about their understanding of the process and their level

---

[3] A maximum likelihood estimation procedure (Davey, Fan, & Reckase, 1996) has been developed that directly estimates the scale point without the need for a separate information weighting step.

of confidence in the results. Overall, panelists endorsed the process and supported the use of the results.

However, not all panelists agreed with the final values corresponding to the boundaries of the achievement-level categories. The distributions in Figure 2 show that there is spread in the estimates provided by panelists. Although it would be desirable to have tight distributions of estimates, ACT staff were careful to indicate that consensus was not required. The message was that consensus was desirable, but honest disagreement was acceptable.

In addition to internal reviews of the process, ACT performed additional studies for previous content areas to show that the achievement-level descriptions were consistent with the ratings and the conditional probability of correct responses for items at various points along the NAEP scale. These validation studies have generally supported the viability of the process. However, the process is judgmental. Exact agreement among panelists was not expected.

SUMMARY

The process for translating NAGB's policy definitions to the NAEP scale is a complex, 6-day exercise that has been well tested through use on a variety of content areas and has been carefully reviewed by numerous outside parties. Although there is professional disagreement on the appropriate means for setting the boundary points for the achievement levels on the NAEP scale or whether there should be achievement levels at all, the process has provided relatively stable results, as indicated by small standard errors and results that are supported by the panelists. In short, the panelists are able to confidently do the required tasks, the mapping process works within the constraints set by NAGB and the NAEP assessment methodology, and the process functions within the same assumptions that are used to estimate performance for the examinee sample on the NAEP scale.

ACKNOWLEDGMENTS

This article was prepared under Contract ZA93003001 with the NAGB for the Committee on the Evaluation of National and State Assessments of Educational Progress. The original version was presented at the NAEP Achievement Levels: Setting Consensus Goals for Academic Achievement workshop, Washington, DC, December 1996.

I had only a small part in the development of the process described in this article. NAGB staff, technical advisors to the project, and others participated in the design process. In particular, Susan Cooper Loomis, Luz Bay, and Lee Chen led the design efforts and had responsibility for implementing the process for NAEP science. The views expressed are solely my own.

REFERENCES

Allen, N. L., Johnson, E. G., Mislevy, R. J., & Thomas, N. (1996). Scaling procedures. In N. L. Allen, D. L. Kline, & C. A. Zelenak (Eds.), *The NAEP 1994 technical report.* Washington, DC: National Center for Educational Statistics.

American College Testing. (1993). *Setting achievement levels on the 1992 National Assessment of Educational Progress in mathematics, reading, and writing: A technical report on reliability and validity.* Iowa City, IA: Author.

American College Testing. (1994, April). *Design document: Setting achievement levels on the 1994 National Assessment of Educational Progress in geography and in U.S. history and the 1996 National Assessment of Educational Progress in science.* Iowa City, IA: Author.

American College Testing. (1997). *Setting achievement levels on the 1996 National Assessment of Educational Progress in science* (Final Report). Iowa City, IA: Author.

Davey, T., Fan, M., & Reckase, M. D. (1996, April). *Some new methods for mapping ratings to the NAEP theta scale to support estimation of NAEP achievement level boundaries.* Paper presented at the annual meeting of the National Council on Measurement in Education, New York.

Lord, F. M. (1980). *Applications of item response theory to practical testing problems.* Hillsdale, NJ: Lawrence Erlbaum Associates, Inc.

Muraki, E. (1992). A generalized partial credit model: Applications of an EM algorithm. *Applied Psychological Measurement, 16,* 159–176.

National Assessment Governing Board. (1995). *Developing student performance levels for the national assessment of educational progress policy statement.* Washington, DC: Author.

National Assessment Governing Board. (1996). *Science framework for the 1996 national assessment of educational progress.* Washington, DC: Author.

Validating Inferences From National Assessment of Educational Progress Achievement-Level Reporting

Robert L. Linn
Center for Research on Evaluation, Standards, and Student Testing
University of Colorado at Boulder

The validity of interpretations of National Assessment of Educational Progress (NAEP) achievement levels is evaluated by focusing on evidence regarding 3 types of discrepancies: (a) discrepancies between standards implied by judgments of different types of items (e.g., multiple choice vs. short answer or dichotomously scored vs. extended response tasks scored using multipoint rubrics), (b) discrepancies between descriptions of achievement levels with their associated exemplar items and the location of cut scores on the scale, and (c) discrepancies between the assessments and content standards. Large discrepancies of all 3 types raise serious questions about some of the more expansive inferences that have been made in reporting NAEP results in terms of achievement levels. It is argued that the evidence reviewed provides a strong case for making more modest inferences and interpretations of achievement levels than have frequently been made.

There is broad professional consensus that it is the uses and interpretations or inferences made from specific uses of assessment results that are validated. As stated in the Test Standards (American Education Research Association, American Psychological Association, and the National Council on Measurement on Education [AERA, APA, NCME], 1985), for example, "[t]he inferences regarding specific uses of tests are validated, not the test itself" (p. 9). In a similar vein, Messick (1989) states: "What is validated is not the test or observation device as such but the inferences derived from test scores or other indicators—inferences

---

Requests for reprints should be sent to Robert L. Linn, Campus Box 249, University of Colorado, Boulder, CO 80309–0249. E-mail: linnr@spot.colorado.edu

about score meaning or interpretation and about the implication for action that the interpretation entails" (p. 13).

I begin with this presumably familiar observation about what is validated for two reasons. First, it makes obvious the importance of attending to the specific uses and interpretations of assessment results when validity is considered. Second, it provides the basis for focusing attention in validation work on performance standards used to report and interpret assessment results.

My remarks are framed in terms of a particular assessment program, the National Assessment of Educational Progress (NAEP). Many of the observations are applicable, however, to other large-scale assessment programs that use performance standards as a way of reporting and interpreting assessment results and that emphasize aggregate results rather than the performance of individual students. Additional issues arise in assessment programs that use performance standards to interpret the performance of and make decisions about individual students. The discussion here, however, is limited to the use of performance standards to report and interpret the performance of groups of students.

NAEP ACHIEVEMENT LEVELS

The National Assessment Governing Board (NAGB) began its effort to report results in terms of performance standards with the 1990 mathematics assessment. The decision to develop and use performance standards to report NAEP results was made by the then newly established governing board. The performance standards that were established by NAGB were named "achievement levels."

The decision to report NAEP results in terms of achievement levels was based on the NAGB's interpretation of the legislation that reauthorized NAEP. Among other responsibilities, the legislation assigned NAGB the responsibility of "identifying appropriate achievement goals" (Augustus F. Hawkins–Robert T. Stafford Elementary and Secondary School Improvement Amendments, 1988). As was noted by the National Academy of Education (NAE) Panel on the Evaluation of the NAEP Trial State Assessment (Shepard, Glaser, Linn, & Bohrnstedt, 1993), the Board

> might have responded in different ways. Given the emerging consensus for establishing national education standards, the fact that the Education Summit was silent on who should set standards, and the fact that NAEP was the only national assessment of achievement based on defensible samples, NAGB interpreted the authorizing legislation as a mandate to set performance standards, which it named "achievement levels," for NAEP. (p. xviii)

Because of the potential importance of the achievement levels in the context of the press for national standards, the 1990 achievement levels were subjected to several evaluations (e.g., Linn, Koretz, Baker, & Burstein, 1991; Stufflebeam, Jaeger, & Scriven, 1991; U.S. General Accounting Office, 1993). NAGB was responsive to many of the criticisms of the evaluators and undertook another, more extensive standard setting effort for the 1992 mathematics and reading assessments. Evaluations of the 1992 effort (e.g., Burstein et al., 1993, 1995–1996; Shepard, 1995; Shepard et al., 1993), however, were again quite critical. The NAE panel, for example, concluded that the achievement levels may reduce rather than enhance the validity of interpretations of NAEP results. Not all agreed. Indeed, there were strong defenders of the 1992 mathematics achievement levels, the process used to set them, and the interpretations that they were intended to support (e.g., American College Testing, 1993; Cizek, 1993; Kane, 1993).

There is no need to review in any detail the controversy that has surrounded the achievement levels since they were first introduced on a trial basis for the 1990 mathematics assessment. There are two points worth making in this context, however. First, the controversy, at least in part, led to a conference on standard setting for large-scale assessments that was held in October 1994 under the joint sponsorship of NAGB and the National Center for Education Statistics (NCES). Although the conference did not resolve the controversy, several of the articles, which are now available in the conference proceedings (NAGB & NCES, 1995), addressed validation issues for performance standards and contributed to the formulation of validity research needs discussed later. Second, much of the criticism revolved around a few critical validity questions that should continue to demand attention in any serious validation effort. I will emphasize three of those questions.

The three validity questions that I consider central to the controversy all involve discrepancies: (a) discrepancies between standards implied by judgments of different types of items (e.g., multiple choice vs. short answer or dichotomously scored vs. extended response tasks scored using multipoint rubrics), (b) discrepancies between descriptions of achievement levels with their associated exemplar items and the location of cutscores on the scale, and (c) discrepancies between the assessments and content standards. Large discrepancies between the level at which judges would set standards when reviewing the multiple-choice, short-answer items and extended-response tasks raise serious questions about the conceptual coherence of the judgments. Discrepancies between descriptions of achievement levels and the location of the cutscore create a mismatch between what students with scores in the range of the scale corresponding to a given achievement level are said to be able to do and what it is that they actually did on the assessment. Finally, a misalignment between performance and content standards on the one hand and assessments and cutscores on the other undermines the construct validity of the intended interpretations of the assessment results. Although the latter discrepancy is most commonly illustrated in the area of mathematics, where comparisons are made between the assessment and the standards published in *Curriculum and Evaluation Standards for School Mathematics* (National Council of Teachers of Mathematics, 1989), the validity concern is obviously a much broader one and should be addressed in developing a validity argument (Kane, 1992) in any subject matter area.

VALIDITY FRAMEWORK

Much of the debate about achievement levels has focused on the standard setting method. This is hardly surprising given that the NAE panel recommended against the use of "the Angoff method or any other item-judgment method to set achievement levels" because the panel concluded that such methods are "fundamentally flawed" (Shepard, et al., 1993, p. 132). Although the method used clearly makes a difference in the outcome—a point that no one seems to dispute[1]—focus on method too often does not come to grips with the fundamental questions of validity of associated interpretations. Instead, the point is made that that there is no "right" answer. Mehrens (1995), for example, stated "Standards are judgmental; there is no right answer as to where a standard should be set" (p. 254). Zieky (1995) made the same point: "We have learned that there is NO 'true' standard that the application of the right method, in the right way, with enough people, will find" (p. 29). I agree with the conclusions as stated by Mehrens and Zieky, but it should not be assumed, as it seems some may have, that this implies either (a) there is therefore no need to obtain evidence to support the validity of uses and interpretations of the standards, or (b) one method is as good as another.

The quality of methods can be distinguished on many grounds. Brennan (1995), for example, suggested that replicability of results as a criterion for evaluating methods and notes how generalizability analyses with items, judges, and occasions as facets can be used in evaluating the quality of method. Similarly, Mehrens (1995) relied on the criteria of ease of use and psychometric properties of the standard (mainly interjudge consistency) in arguing for the Angoff method as his preferred method. Two of the three criteria used by Kane (1995) to compare "task-centered

---

[1]Shepard, Glaser, Linn, and Bohrnstedt (1993), for example, concluded that "[t]he most consistent finding from the research literature on standard setting is that different methods lead to different results" (p. 24). Berk (1995) stated it even more strongly: "Probably the only point of agreement among standard setting gurus is that there is hardly any agreement between results of any two standard-setting methods, even when applied to the same test under seemingly identical conditions" (p. 162).

approaches" (e.g., the Angoff method) with "examinee-centered approaches" were also of a similar nature "practical feasibility in the context" and "technical considerations in the context" (p. 130).

There is a substantial literature on methods of setting standards. There is considerable information available to guide the selection and training of judges, the use of multiple judgment rounds, and the introduction of impact data. Comparative studies where different methods are used yield different standards (e.g., see Mehrens, 1995). There is much less information about the psychological demands of different judgment procedures on judges or on the degree to which different methods are likely to differ in the validity of interpretations of results.

Method differences in interjudge consistency or in other components of a generalizability study (e.g., occasions or subsets of items judged) are certainly relevant to an overall evaluation of validity, but they do not address core validity issues. Just as the most reliable test need not be the one that supports the most valid inferences about students, the method that yields the most replicable standards or the standards with the highest interjudge consistency need not produce the standards that yield the most valid interpretations of student achievement.

A common criticism of psychometricians is that although we all give lip service to the doctrine that "validity is the most important consideration in test evaluation" (AERA, APA, & NCME, 1985, p. 9), we too often act in other ways, giving more attention to easier jobs of evaluating and enhancing reliability at the expense of the more difficult jobs of evaluating and enhancing validity (e.g., see Gipps, 1994, p. 76). This criticism also seems to fit much of the work on the development and evaluation of performance standards. Too little attention has been given to the interpretations associated with standards and the validity of interpretations in comparison to the amount of attention given to technique, interjudge consistency, and lack of consistency across methods.

There are, of course, exceptions. Kane's (1995) first criterion for comparing task-centered and examinee-centered standard setting methods, for example, concerned the consistency of the methods with the "model of achievement" underlying the design of the assessment. Kane argued that "all aspects of an assessment program, including test development, scoring, standard setting, and reporting of results, should be consistent with the intended interpretation of the results" (p. 121). He concluded that holistic models of learning and achievement are more compatible with examinee-centered methods whereas analytic models are more compatible with task-centered methods. Kane indicated that such an analysis was not conclusive with regard to NAEP because both models have adherents in the NAEP context, and there is some reason to believe that NAEP may be in a state of transition from a dominant analytic model to greater emphasis on a holistic model. The key point for present purposes, however, is that such an analysis usefully focuses attention on the achievement construct that the assessment is intended to measure. This seems the proper place to begin a serious consideration of validity of standards-based interpretations of assessment results.

The previously mentioned discrepancies in the location of the standard implied by judgments of different types of items is relevant in this regard. Item type represents method variance that is a potential source of invalidity in the location of cutscores in relation to the performance standard constructs. The discrepancies in cutscores as a function of item type reported by Shepard et al. (1993) were quite large in both reading and mathematics at all three grade levels and all three achievement levels. The largest of the discrepancies between cutscores based on different item types at a given grade and achievement level were larger than the differences between cutscores between grades or levels when the same item type was being judged. For example, at Grade 4 in mathematics, the basic-level cutscore based on right–wrong items was 190.4, which would have resulted in 78% of the fourth graders being classified as basic or above. The corresponding cutscores at Grades 8 and 12 were 232.5 and 249.9, respectively. Both of the latter cutscores are lower than the cutscore of 281.1 for the Grade 4 basic level based on reviews of the extended response items, a level that would have led to only 3% of the fourth-grade students being classified as basic. Such huge discrepancies led the NAE panel to conclude that "the extreme differences between cutpoints based on right–wrong items and extended-response items argue strongly that the judges are unable to maintain a consistent view of borderline performance for each of the levels" (Shepard et al., 1993, p. 54).

Such differences contributed to the NAE panel's rejection of the Angoff method of setting standards. Kane (1995) countered that it would seem "more reasonable to reject the results of the extended-response items, which ... may have been subject to bias due to a nonrepresentative sample of student papers" (pp. 126–127). The direction of the difference, however, was the same in 18 comparisons (two subjects, three grades, and three achievement levels). Moreover, subsequent results for the achievement levels in the 1994 assessments in geography and U.S. history, while less dramatic than those in the 1992 assessments in reading and mathematics are also in the same general direction (Glaser, Linn, & Bohrnstedt, 1996). This tendency is illustrated in Figure 1, where distributions of scores and achievement levels are displayed for the 1994 Grade 12 geography and U.S. history assessments.

The box-and-whisker plots in Figure 1 show the distributions of Grade 12 scores on the 1994 geography and U.S. history assessments. The levels at which three achievement levels were set are displayed by the horizontal lines to the right of each of the box-and-whisker plots. The vertical lines to the right of the box-and-whisker plots show the extremes between where the cutscore would be set based on the judgments of extended-response items and where they would be set based only on dichotomous items. In each case, the upper end of the range of possible cutscores always corresponds to the point for extended-response items and the lower end to dichotomously scored, right–wrong items. The results in Figure 1 reinforce my

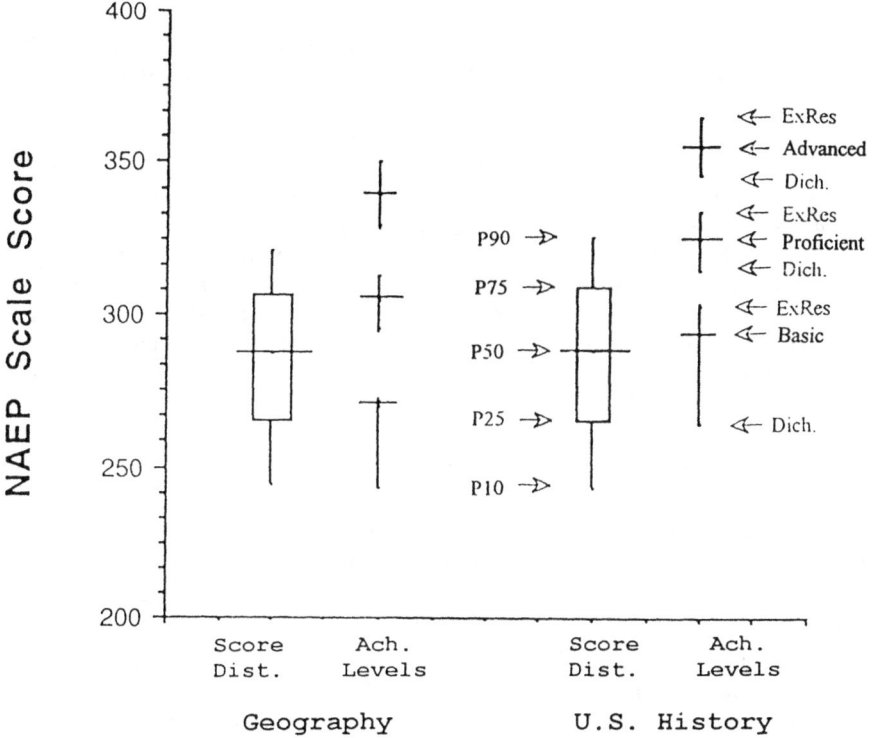

FIGURE 1 Score distributions and achievement levels (actual and item type) for the 1994 National Assessment of Education Progress Grade 12 assessments in geography and U.S. history.

belief that there is substantial method variance caused by item format that contributes to the invalidity of the achievement levels by making the location of the cutscore depend on the particular mix of item types that happens to be in the set reviewed by judges in a given year.

CONTENT STANDARDS, THE ACHIEVEMENT CONSTRUCT, AND PERFORMANCE STANDARDS

Messick (1995) argued that

> the validity of content and performance standards cannot be separated from the validity of the assessment itself or of its measurement scale. Therefore, the validity of standards must be addressed in terms of the same criteria needed to appraise the validity of assessments generally. (p. 302)

No one familiar with Messick's (e.g., 1989) extensive writings on the topic of validity would be surprised to learn that this means that he thought that construct validation issues should be paramount. In particular, he stated the issue as follows:

> to address the construct validity of both content standards and performance standards, the same framework of validity criteria and forms of evidence must be used as are needed to appraise the construct validity of the assessed student competence. This is necessary because the construct validity of the content standards and the construct validity of the measurement scales go hand in hand. Moreover, to be meaningfully interpreted and reported, both the assessed competence and the performance standard must be described in the same **construct** terms. That is, a performance standard has two critical aspects: its location on the measurement scale and its meaning in terms of the nature or quality of the knowledge or skill characterizing proficiency at that level. (Messick, 1995, p. 291)

The formulation of validity issues related to performance standards in terms of the broad construct validation framework is conceptually appealing. I have no quarrel with that as a starting point. Leaving it at that, however, has the potential problem that Shepard (1993) noted with regard to Messick's (1989) most general treatment of validity. Because of the very comprehensiveness and complexity of the formulation, "it does not help to identify which validity questions are essential to support a test use" (p. 427)—in this case, the interpretation of NAEP results in terms of achievement levels. Shepard argued that validators need to prioritize validity questions and suggested that a way to do this was to start with the claims made in a use or interpretation of results.

Shepard (1993) suggested that, like a good evaluator, a validator needs to identify priority questions by listening "both to affirmative claims and to program critics" (p. 434; see also Cronbach, 1988, 1989). She illustrated how priority questions can be identified and addressed in four specific testing programs making use of Kane's (1992) argument-based approach to validation. According to Kane (1992) "the argument-based approach to validity is basically quite simple. One chooses the interpretation, specifies the interpretive argument associated with the interpretation, identifies competing interpretations, and develops evidence to support the intended interpretation and to refute the competing interpretations" (p. 53).

APPLICATION TO NAEP ACHIEVEMENT LEVELS

I believe that Messick's (1995) formulation of the validity issues for performance standards provides a needed conceptual framework. There needs to be a way of moving from the abstract theoretical framework to specific questions and evidence most relevant to evaluating claims and counterclaims about the interpretation of results reported in terms of achievement levels. The argument-based approach to validation discussed by Cronbach (1988, 1989), Kane (1992), and Shepard (1993) provided a useful way of taking that step from the abstract to a practical program of validity research because it provided a way of organizing and prioritizing the validity questions and related research. To illustrate this approach to validating achievement levels, I begin with the intended interpretive uses of the achievement levels.

Two major interpretive uses of achievement levels may be distinguished. One use is to try to impart substantive meaning to scaled scores. This use is not different in kind from the earlier use of anchor points that were intended to give meaning to scale scores by describing the nature of performance required to score at the arbitrarily chosen anchor points (e.g., 200, 250, 300) and by illustrating performance at those points with anchor items (i.e., items that students scoring at that level had a relatively high probability of answering correctly but students scoring at the next lower anchor point were less likely to answer correctly).[2] Although, as others have noted (e.g., Lissitz & Bourque, 1995), the anchor points were never subjected to the same level of scrutiny as the achievement levels have been, the validity issues for this intended use as a means of giving substantive meaning to selected levels of performance on the NAEP scale are essentially the same.

The second major interpretive use intended for the achievement levels is more clearly evaluative in character. That is, the use of the standards as a means of indicating what performance is expected, or what students should be able to do. This evaluative interpretation distinguishes the achievement levels from the earlier anchor points. To be sure, anchor points were used in clearly evaluative ways by commentators (e.g., Shanker, 1990) and in earlier applications by choice of single word descriptors of the anchor points (e.g., characterizing the highest anchor point as the "adept" level) or in the verbal characterizations of student performance. In their summary of the first 20 years of NAEP results published before any attempt to set achievement levels had been completed, for example, Mullis, Dossey, Owen, and Phillips (1990) concluded that "Large proportions, perhaps more than half, of our elementary, middle school, and high school students are unable to demonstrate competency in challenging subject matter in English, Mathematics, Science, History, and Geography" (p. 29). Several similar examples of evaluative interpretations of results reported in terms of anchor points were discussed (Forsyth, 1991). The evaluative judgment that students at a given level were or were not performing

---

[2]Specifically, an anchor item had to meet three statistical criteria: (a) the proportion correct, or p value, for students within 12.5 points of the anchor point in question (e.g., scores between 237.5 and 262.5 for anchor point 250) had to be greater than or equal .65; (b) the p value for students within 12.5 points of the next lower anchor point (e.g., 200) had to be less than .50; and (c) the difference between the two p values had to be at least 30. In addition, the p values at both levels needed to be based on at least 100 students. Verbal descriptions of the knowledge and understandings were developed by panels based on their review of the assessment objectives and the anchor items to characterize the achievement corresponding to each level (Mullis, Dossey, Owen, & Phillips, 1991, pp. 462–464).

competently, however, was neither an official policy nor an explicit part of the anchor points.

The move to achievement levels explicitly added the evaluative component to the intended interpretation as part of official NAGB policy. The intended shift from only attempting to provide substantive meaning to scale interpretations to an evaluative interpretation is evident in the NAGB's (1991) characterization of the achievement levels in their report on the initial 1990 effort as marking

> a significant departure from prior practice. Previously, NAEP results have only been reported in terms of statistical profiles. Now, for the first time on the national level, the Board's new standards allow NAEP data to be reported in terms of what students *should* be able to do. (p. vii)

EVALUATIVE INTERPRETATION

First, I consider some validity issues related to the second of these major uses of achievement levels. Second, I provide evaluative interpretation of NAEP results, and then turn to the use as an aid in interpreting the substantive meaning of results. The intended evaluative use of achievement levels is clearly stated in the most recent reports of NAEP results. This is illustrated by the following general statement taken from the report of the 1994 NAEP geography assessment results (Persky et al., 1996):

> These levels of student achievement have been established to help Americans answer two questions that are important to parents and to all citizens in the communities and nation in which we live. "What should students know and be able to do as they progress and graduate from school?" and "How good is good enough in terms of student achievement on NAEP?" Answering these questions obviously involves judgments. The National Assessment Governing Board is not suggesting that there is a single answer to these questions. Rather, the Board is trying to put forward reasonable judgments that can inform citizens across America—information they can use to answer these questions in their own schools and communities. (p. 25)

The identical quotation could have been taken from the report of the 1994 NAEP U.S. history assessment results (Beatty, Reese, Persky, & Carr, 1996, p. 29). The report of the reading assessment results, the remaining content area assessed by NAEP in 1994, did not include that statement but instead gave the following general characterization of the potential utility of the achievement levels:

> The reading proficiency of our nation's students can be explored further by considering the proportion of students who attained specific achievement levels established by the National Assessment Governing Board (NAGB) in 1992 for the current reading assessment framework. Viewing reading performance from this perspective provides

TABLE 1
Policy Definitions of 1994 National Assessment of Educational Progress
Achievement Levels

Basic	This level denotes partial mastery of prerequisite knowledge and skills that are fundamental for proficient work at each grade.
Proficient	This level represents solid academic performance for each grade assessed. Students reaching this level have demonstrated competency over challenging subject matter, including subject-matter knowledge, application of such knowledge to real-world situations, and analytical skills appropriate to the subject matter.
Advanced	This level signifies superior performance.

Note. These quoted policy definitions are identical in each of the major reports of the 1994 assessment results, that is, for geography (Figure 1.2 in Persky et al., 1996, p. 6), for history (Figure 1.2 in Beatty, Reese, Persky, & Carr, 1996, p. 6), and for reading (Figure 1.4 in Campbell, Donahue, Reese, & Phillips, 1996).

insight into the adequacy of students' reading abilities and the extent to which they are achieving expected levels of performance. (Campbell, Donahue, Reese, & Phillips, 1996, p. 41)

The expected levels of performance are embodied in three achievement levels—basic, proficient, and advanced—that are converted into three specific cutscores on the NAEP scale through a relatively elaborate judgmental standard setting process at each grade level for each subject. The three cutscores, of course, divide the NAEP scale in a given subject into four regions per grade. The estimated percentage of students scoring below the basic achievement level and the percentages scoring at or above each of the cutscores are reported.

The specific achievement-level descriptions in each subject area and grade level are developed from a common set of definitions for the three achievement levels that are called the policy definitions of the NAEP achievement levels. The policy definitions for the basic, proficient, and advanced levels that were used for the 1994 assessments (reading, geography, and U.S. history) are reproduced in Table 1. Starting with those definitions, panels of judges for each subject area developed content area specific definitions of the levels for each of the three grade levels (4, 8, & 12) assessed by NAEP.

Before considering those more specific descriptions, it is worth noting that the policy definitions used in 1994 evolved from more elaborate generic definitions that were used in the initial achievement-level setting effort that was undertaken for the 1990 mathematics assessment or the ones stated in the 1991 NAGB request for proposals (RFP) for setting the achievement levels for the 1992 NAEP assessments in mathematics, reading, and writing (NAGB, 1991). The definitions of the three levels in the 1991 RFP are shown in Table 2.

As can be seen by comparing the definitions in Tables 1 and 2, the policy definitions for the 1994 assessments were more modest and streamlined than the

TABLE 2
Generic Definitions of Request for Proposals for Setting the 1992 NAEP Achievement Levels in Reading, Mathematics, and Writing

Basic	This level, below proficient, denotes partial mastery of knowledge and skills that are fundamental for the proficient work at each grade—4, 8, and 12. For 12th grade this will be higher than minimum competency skills (which normally are taught in elementary and junior high schools) and will cover significant elements of standard high school-level work.
Proficient	This central level represents solid academic performance for each grade tested—4, 8, and 12. It will reflect a consensus that students reaching this level have demonstrated competency over challenging subject matter and are well prepared for the next level of schooling. For 12th grade the proficient level will encompass a body of subject-matter knowledge and analytical skills, of cultural literacy and insight, that all high school graduates should have for democratic citizenship, responsible adulthood, and productive work.
Advanced	This higher level signifies superior performance beyond proficient grade-level mastery at Grades 4, 8, and 12. For 12th grade the advanced level will show readiness of rigorous college courses, advanced technical training, or employment requiring advanced academic achievement. As data become available, it may be based, in part, on international comparisons of academic achievement and may also be related to Advanced Placement and other college placement exams.

Note. From National Assessment Governing Board. (1991, p. 2). NAEP = National Assessment of Educational Progress.

ones presented in the 1991 RFP. This was used to guide the achievement-level setting process for the 1992 assessments. The implicit validity claims are both more extensive and more difficult to substantiate in the longer 1991 RFP generic statements than in the more recent policy definitions reported for the 1994 assessments.

Some evaluations of the 1990 and 1992 achievement levels (e.g., Linn et al., 1991; Shepard et al., 1993) were critical, in part, on the grounds that there was no evidence to support the implicit predictions in the definitions (e.g., "readiness for rigorous college courses" or skills and insights needed for productive work) or because of evidence that was interpreted to run counter to the claim. Shepard et al., for example, used comparisons of the percentage of students achieving scores of 3 or higher on Advanced Placement examinations (the score level frequently used to award college credit) and the percentage of students obtaining scores of 600 or higher on the Scholastic Aptitude Test (SAT) mathematics test or 550 or higher on the SAT verbal test (levels on the 1992 SAT scales that corresponded to the 86th percentile of test takers on the verbal test and the 82nd percentile on the mathematics test) to argue that a higher percentage of 12th graders perform at the level defined as advanced than are so classified on NAEP.

There is, of course, no gold standard against that to compare the proficient level or the advanced level. This is no different than validation in other contexts. As Cronbach (1980) noted some years ago, "The validity [or, I might add, the lack thereof] cannot be established by a research monograph," but the report should "advance sensible discussion" (p. 106). The statement in the earlier generic definitions of the advanced level (see Table 2) that at Grade 12 "the advanced level will show readiness of rigorous college courses" can reasonably be taken to mean that students scoring below that level are not ready for such courses. Critics of this interpretation of the advanced level point to the fact that only 2% of 12th-grade students were found to be at the advanced level on the 1992 NAEP mathematics assessment (Mullis, Dossey, Owen, & Phillips, 1993, p. 7) and ask how, if so few students are ready for rigorous college level work, 18% of the SAT test takers could score at 600 or higher on the SAT mathematics test. Even making the ultraconservative assumption that none of the high school seniors who did not take the SAT would have scored 600 or higher on the SAT mathematics test if they had taken it, Shepard et al. (1993) estimated that 7.5% of all high school graduates scored above 600. On the other hand, those arguing in defense of the achievement levels respond that there is "ambiguity in what constitutes advanced performance on the SAT" (Kane, 1993, p. 18).

Although it is undoubtedly obvious which side of the argument I am on, the point of this example is not to show how validation research can resolve the issue. Quite the contrary. The example illustrates how the implicit claims in interpretations of the achievement levels can be used to identify evidence to be used in the validity argument. Evidence only rarely speaks for itself in an unambiguous way. It needs to be surrounded by a persuasive argument that "speaks to a diverse and potentially critical audience" (Cronbach, 1988, p. 4).

The interpretive phrase in question for the previous example (i.e., "readiness for rigorous college level courses") has been removed from the policy definition of advanced performance (see Table 1). The leaner statement used for the 1994 reports of achievement levels, "signifies superior performance," has been stripped of the implicit predictions in earlier definitions.

Whether one agrees with the argument, based on comparisons such as the ones just mentioned, that the cutscores are set too high in relation to the defined achievement levels, that type of comparison is clearly in keeping with the development of evidence to evaluate interpretive claims made by the achievement levels. Note, incidentally, that I did not say "too high period," but too high in relation to the stated definition of the level. Merely setting the bar as high as NAGB, or any other group desires, does not, by itself, cause validity problems. Setting the bar at one level and describing performance that corresponds better to quite a different level, however, leads to invalid inferences. It is this latter possibility that demands the attention of validators of the achievement levels.

Because NAGB has backed away from the more elaborate definitions in Table 2 in favor of the more streamlined definitions in Table 1, the specific criticisms that the implicit predictive and comparative claims in Table 2 lack validity may be considered moot. It should be noted, however, that the 1995 National Education

Goals Panel report (NEGP; 1995) in which the 1994 NAEP results are reported continued to use the definitions shown in Table 2, except that the last sentence of the advanced level definition in Table 2 was deleted in the NEGP report (p. 160). More important, the examples remain relevant as illustrations of how the interpretive statements can fruitfully be used to develop a validity argument.

The recent announcement in President Clinton's 1997 State of the Union Address of plans to develop a national test in reading at Grade 4 may substantially increase the importance of the evaluative function of the NAEP achievement levels because it is planned that the national test would be linked to NAEP and have results reported in terms of the achievement levels. A 1997 publication of the Department of Education entitled *A Call to Action for American Education in the 21st Century,* (U.S. Department of Education, 1997) released at the time of Secretary Riley's State of Education Address in Atlanta, Georgia, on February 18, 1997, argued that "more than 40% [of America's fourth graders] cannot read as well as they must to succeed later in school and in the workforce" (p. 2). The 40% figure corresponds to the percentage of fourth-grade students who performed below the basic level in the 1994 NAEP reading assessment (Campbell et al., 1996, p. 61).

The evaluative interpretation in the *A Call to Action for American Education in the 21st Century* would seem to bring back unvalidated predictive interpretations like those in the earlier achievement-level descriptions illustrated in Table 2 that were dropped from the more recent NAEP descriptions. Moreover, the juxtaposition of the result with the argument by President Clinton and the Department of Education that "[w]e must end social promotion: Students should have to show what they've learned to move from grade school to middle school and from middle school to high school" (U.S. Department of Education, 1997, p. 2) raises the stakes, at least rhetorically, for the achievement levels, and if put into action would demand a higher standard of validity evidence.

SUBSTANTIVE INTERPRETATIONS

The evaluative interpretation that achievement levels are intended to provide is obviously an important use that needs to be attended to in validation efforts. As was noted previously, however, that is not the only use. Achievement levels are also supposed to enhance the substantive meaning of results. That is, the descriptions are supposed to provide a means of knowing what students at a given level understand and are likely to be able to do so. The substantive interpretations in essence make claims that demand additional validity evidence.

Shepard (1995) stated this additional demand:

> If the only purpose of standards is to "sound the alarm" that too many students are falling below desired levels of achievement, then simple quantifications or cut scores

alone would be sufficient. However, if standards are intended to give meaning to the assessment and show what students should be able to do, then more substantive performance standards are needed. To set expectations, standards should embody or represent what students must know to attain the standard. On NAEP the achievement level descriptions and accompanying exemplar items were intended to convey what was expected at each level. (p. 145)

The fourth grade descriptions of the proficient achievement level are shown in Table 3 for the three subject areas (geography, U.S. history, and reading) assessed in 1994. To be considered proficient in any of the three subjects, students are clearly expected to know and be qualified to do a lot. The descriptions invite a correspondingly large array of inferences about the understandings, skills, and abilities that students who score at or above the minimum score for the proficient level at Grade 4 must posses. One would reasonably infer that a student who is proficient in

TABLE 3
Proficient Achievement Level Descriptions at Grade 4 for the Three Subject Areas Assessed in 1994 (Geography, U.S. History, and Reading)

Geography	Students should be able to use fundamental geographic knowledge and vocabulary to identify basic geographic patterns and processes; describe an environmental or cultural issue from more than one perspective; and read and interpret information from visual and technological tools such as photographs, maps and globes, aerial photography, and satellite images. They should be able to use number and letter grids to plot specific locations; understand relative location terms; and sketch simple maps and describe and/or draw landscapes they have observed or studied. Proficient students should be able to illustrate how people depend upon, adapt to, and modify the environment, describe and/or illustrate geographic aspects of a region using fundamental geographic vocabulary and give reasons for current human migration; discuss the impact a location has upon cultural similarities and differences; and be able to demonstrate how an event in one location can have an impact upon another location. (Persky et al., 1996, p. 26)
U.S. history	Fourth-grade students performing at the Proficient level should be able to identify, describe and comment on the significance of many historical people, places, ideas, events, and documents. They should interpret information from a variety of sources, including texts, maps, pictures, and timelines. They should be able to construct a simple timeline from data. These students should recognize the role of invention and technological change in history. They should also recognize the ways in which geographic and environmental factors have influenced life and work. (Beatty, Reese, Persky, & Carr, 1996, p. 30)
Reading	Fourth-grade students performing at the Proficient level should be able to demonstrate an overall understanding of the text, providing inferential as well as literal information. When reading text appropriate to fourth grade, they should be able to extend the ideas in the text by making inferences, drawing conclusions, and making connections to their own experiences. The connection between the text and what the student infers should be clear. (Campbell, Donahue, Reese, & Phillips, 1996, p. 42)

geography, for example, would be able to read and interpret a map, an aerial photograph, or a satellite image. Hence, an important validity question is the extent to which such inferences are justified.

Saying that a proficient student can read and interpret maps sounds like a criterion-referenced interpretation as originally described by Glaser (1963). As Forsyth (1991) indicated, it was also true of the descriptions and anchor items that were used in an effort to explain what students scoring near the anchor points could do. The type of analysis that Forsyth did with respect to the criterion-referenced interpretations based on anchor points is equally relevant to the parallel interpretations of the achievement levels. Indeed because a good deal of Forsyth's argument focused on the NAEP scales rather than the specific points on the scales where the anchor points were located, much of his argument is directly applicable to the achievement levels.

Of particular relevance to validity arguments regarding the substantive interpretations of performance provided by the achievement-level descriptions is Forsyth's (1991) claim that the NAEP domains are too broad and too ill defined to support criterion-referenced interpretations. One of the appealing features of item response theory (IRT) is, of course, the ordering of people and assessment items on the same IRT scale. Unfortunately, however, the IRT ordering of items does not necessarily correspond to any ordering of items implied by the substantive descriptions of achievement levels.

Achievement levels are set for the composite scales in each subject area. But the items are drawn from content by process matrices, and the composite scales are weighted combinations of separate IRT scales for the content area. The composite scale for the 1994 geography assessment, for example, is a weighted combination of three IRT content area scales (space and place, environment and society, and spatial dynamics and connections), and each of the content areas is made up of a combination of items across three *cognitive dimensions* (knowing, understanding, and applying). For the 1994 U.S. history assessment, the composite score is a weighted average across four historical themes[3] with items drawn from eight historical periods (e.g., 1607–1763).

Forsyth (1991) argued that the mixing of dimensions was problematic for the criterion-reference interpretations of the anchor points. "This mixing would not be so critical if NAEP did not claim that this scale permits us to describe specifically what individuals can do" (p. 6). It is argued that the descriptions of anchor points made the implicit claim that the results could be interpreted in criterion-referenced

---

[3]The four themes are (a) change and continuity in American democracy: ideas, institutions, practices, and controversies; (b) the gathering and interactions of peoples, cultures, and ideas; (c) economic and technological changes and their relation to society, ideas, and the environment; and (d) the changing role of America in the world.

terms. Forsyth concluded, "without reservations" (p. 9), however, that such an interpretation is simply invalid. In my judgment, the interpretive use of achievement-level descriptions for the composite NAEP scales invite the same type of criterion-reference interpretation that Forsyth criticized. Hence, validity arguments regarding achievement levels need to address the issues raised by Forsyth with regard to the description of anchor points.

Millman (1994) argued that NAEP assessments "are just not designed to provide, nor do they claim to provide, the promised CR [criterion-referenced] interpretation (see Forsyth, 1991, on this point)" (p. 20). He noted that although some example items and associated items statistics are reported for NAEP, "elusive constructs such as the ability to 'identify extraneous information,' 'list the possible arrangements in a sample space,' and 'solve the length of missing segments in more complex situations' (Mullis et al., 1993, pp. 236–237) dominate" (p. 20).

Millman (1994) proceeded to ask whether the introduction of achievement-level reporting would add to the criterion-referenced interpretation of NAEP results, and answered his own question in this regard with a simple "no." He provided the following rationale for his negative answer:

> Determining that a student is at a proficient level in a subject—reading, for example—does not give us a confident assessment of the specific tasks a student can or cannot do. Although the achievement levels are defined in terms of groups of "elusive constructs," previously illustrated, performance on tasks measuring such constructs can span the achievement scale. (p. 39)

EXEMPLAR ITEMS AND ITEM MAPPING

The descriptions of achievement levels can be parsed into a series of statements that seem to correspond to possible assessment items. For example, in U.S. history the Grade 4 proficient student "should be able to describe ... many ... historical ... events," "to construct a simple timeline from data," and "recognize the ways in which geographic ... factors have influenced life and work" (Beatty, Reese, Persky, & Carr, 1996, p. 30; see Table 3). These are just a few of the "shoulds" at this level. It is also the case that each of these relatively specific shoulds could be operationalized by a host of different assessment items or tasks. Which historical events should be described? What constitutes an adequate description of an event? What proportion adequately described constitutes many?

One way of responding to such questions is to provide exemplar items to illustrate the more general statements in the description. That approach was taken, for example, with the 1992 mathematics achievement levels. The published exemplar items (Mullis et al., 1993) were selected to illustrate the verbal descriptions of the levels. However, some of them were not answered correctly by even a simple majority of the students scoring at the level the item was intended to exemplify (Burstein et al., 1995–96). At Grade 8, the description of the proficient level states that students at that level "should make inferences for data and graphs" (Mullis et al., 1993, p. 51). One of the Grade 8 exemplar items presented students with a graph showing a scatterplot of number of sit-ups with age in years accompanied by a multiple choice question asking the median number of sit-ups for the 13 people represented in the graph (Mullis et al., 1993, p. 54). Although that would appear to be a reasonable example to help make the achievement-level description more concrete, only 36% of the eighth-grade students scoring in the proficient range answered that item correctly. For a brief time, such discrepancies led to some rather silly and convoluted discussions saying that the achievement levels indicated only what students should be able to do, not necessarily what students who achieve at those levels actually can do. Such a position simply is not tenable. One cannot simultaneously have a large sample of students at the proficient level and yet have a majority of those students be unable to answer correctly items selected to be operational exemplars of the proficient level. Furthermore, the review of statements in the print media about performance in terms of achievement levels by Koretz and Deibert (1995–96) clearly shows, not surprisingly, that the press "interpreted NAEP's presentation of achievement levels as statements about what students actually can do" (p. 70).

Levels may be determined by focusing on the should question, but once determined, the whole purpose of the assessment is to learn what students actually do, and achievement-level descriptions and exemplar items need to help convey as accurately as possible what students performing at a given level know and are able to do. Otherwise, they mislead rather than add meaning to the interpretation of student performance.

Another difficulty with the 1992 exemplar items in mathematics was that on some of the items a substantial majority of students performing below the level the item was said to exemplify actually got the item right (Burstein et al., 1995–96). Indeed, on statistical grounds some of the exemplars for the proficient, or even the advanced, level were similar to some of the exemplars for the basic level. At Grade 4, for example, a total of 10 exemplar items were reported—2 basic, 5 proficient, and 3 advanced exemplars. The proportions correct for 5 of those 10 exemplar items are shown in Figure 2 for students scoring in each of the score ranges defined by the three achievement levels. As can be seen, a slightly larger proportion of students scoring at the basic level answered the advanced level exemplar correctly than answered the second basic level exemplar correctly. The exemplar with the largest proportion correct for students at the basic performance level was one of the proficient exemplars shown in Figure 2, not, as one would expect, one of the two basic exemplars.

The problem illustrated in Figure 2 was corrected when items were selected as exemplars for the 1992 reading assessment. Exemplars were then required to meet

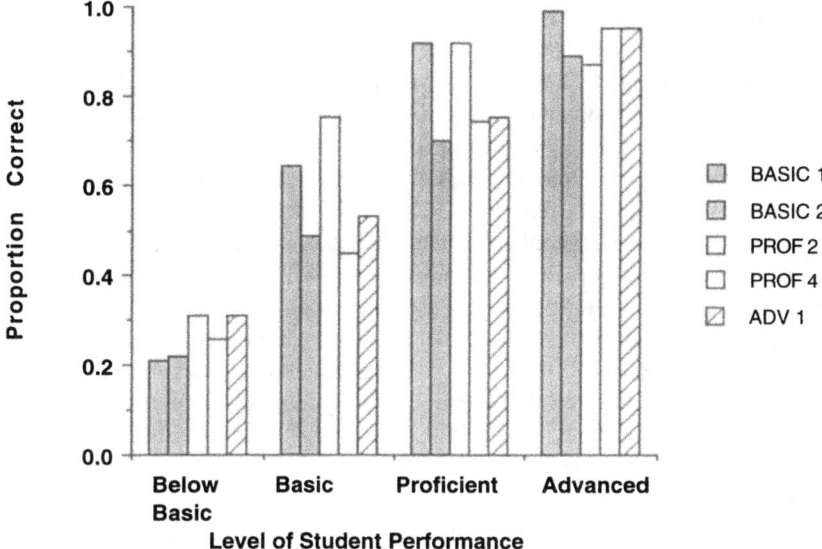

FIGURE 2 Proportion correct by achievement level for Grade 4 exemplar items selected to illustrate proficient and advanced exemplars that are statistically similar to basic exemplars (see Burstein, et al., 1995–96, Table 2, p. 19).

both the judgmental criteria that they were thought to be good illustrations of the achievement-level descriptions and statistical criteria. So why dwell on ancient history? There are two answers to that question. First, the example, like the one discussed earlier regarding implicit predictions in statements about readiness for rigorous college courses, illustrates how validation work can lead to modifications of practice that change the nature of inferences that need to be validated. Second, the example provides needed background for considering the next validity issue.

In keeping with the addition of statistical criteria for exemplar items used for the 1992 reading assessment, Brennan (1995) observed that the choice of exemplars usually depends on some statistical criterion, for example, "the probability is at least X that examinees at every score level in a range of scores get the item correct ... [obviously] the choice of X can have a substantial impact on the final exemplars chosen" (p. 280). Brennan continued to note that the rationale for choosing X should be made explicit and cautions against common misinterpretations (e.g., all proficient examinees can do this item). We are short of rationales for choice of any particular X, although one may be hard pressed to argue seriously for something lower than .50. We are shorter still on evidence regarding the validity of inferences that are made based on the presentation of exemplars with different X's. To be considered a reasonable exemplar, both the choice of X for examinees in the score range, and the choice of Y, the maximum probability of correct responses for students scoring at a substantially lower level should be examined. The advanced exemplar item in Figure 2, for example, not only meets an X greater than .50 for students scoring in the advanced range but also meets that criterion for students in the proficient range and students in the basic range.

Exemplar items for each of the achievement levels were not included in the 1994 reports for geography, reading, or U.S. history. Instead, example items are given along with the percentage of all students who answered the item correctly or achieved a specified score or higher on extended response items that are scored on more than zero-one score rubrics (e.g., the percentage with score of 3 or higher on a 4-point scoring rubric). Also presented are the conditional percentages correct (or scored at or above the specified rubric score) for each of the four achievement-level intervals. The percentages are reported separately for students scoring in the below basic, the basic, the proficient, and the advanced intervals. The items are not associated with an achievement-level as they were with the earlier exemplar items, however.

Descriptors of items are also mapped to the scale score for each subscale. The mapping is done by assigning the score to an item that corresponds to the point at which a specified percentage of students performed satisfactorily on the item (i.e., gave correct answers for dichotomously scored items and obtained a score of, say, 3 or higher on an item with 4-point scoring rubric). The specified percentage is 65 for free-response items and 74 for multiple-choice items.

The reported items that map into the Grade 4 proficient interval on the 1994 U.S. history assessment are listed in Table 4 for each of the four U.S. history theme scales. A number of validity questions are raised by the item maps. For example, What is the justification for the choice of X = 65% for free-response and 74% for multiple-choice items? How well do the items mapped into a given achievement-level interval correspond to the description of that level? How well is the distinction made between the items mapped into one achievement-level interval and the description of another achievement level? How adequate are the labels for items in the maps for conveying a sense of the tasks that students in that interval correctly answer with probability greater than X?

With regard to the last of these illustrative questions, it seems clear that any of the item labels (e.g., "place immigrant quotation in historical context") could, in fact, fit many different items. The probabilities of a right answer depend heavily on the particular question (e.g., what immigrant quotation). They also depend on the distractors and precise wording of the right answer if it is a multiple-choice question and on the scoring criteria if it is an open-ended question. Thus, although the item labels are closer to the actual assessment tasks than the achievement-level descriptions because they are each tied to an actual item on the assessment, there is still a large gap between labels and any rigorous understanding of what it is that students in a given score interval actually can do with probability greater than X.

TABLE 4
Map of Selected Items on the U.S. History Theme Subscales for Grade 4 That Are Mapped into the Proficient Level Range of Scores (243–175)

Range	Items
Theme Scale 1: Change and continuity in American democracy: Ideas, institutions, practices, and controversies	
275	Identify purpose of Bill of Rights
266	Recognize result of Boston Tea Party
262	Identify one of the 13 colonies that fought Revolution
259	Interpret and identify historical context for African American voter registration charts
258	Provide accurate facts about famous figure in American history charts
251	Recognize reason why Pilgrims and Puritans came to America
247	Place House Divided Speech in historical context
Theme Scale 2: The gathering and interactions of peoples, cultures, and ideas	
273	Identify causal significance of Columbus's voyages for Europe
271	Describe why Pilgrims celebrated first Thanksgiving
268	Place immigrant quotation in historical context
268	Infer from drawing of American Indian village how inhabitants got food
256	Identify American Indian tribe that followed the Trail of Tears
252	Identify Oregon Trail
247	Locate birthplace of slaves on world map
244	Identify significance of Drinking Gourd song sung by slaves
Theme Scale 3: Economic and technological changes and their relation to society, ideas, and the environment	
269	Infer from diary entry differences between 18th century and contemporary children's lives
267	Recognize purpose of labor unions
263	Explain how modern inventions would change life described in 18th century diary
261	Analyze how electronic inventions changed lives
247	Understand why early mills were built on water
247	Recognize what product label says about U.S. economy
Theme Scale 4: The changing role of America in the world	
260	Distinguish Vietnam as longest war on list
256	Interpret appeal of army recruiting poster
246	Identify Columbus's intended destination in 1492
245	List three important facts about famous site

Note. From Beatty, Reese, Persky, and Carr (1996, pp. 80–81). The numbers give the point on the subscale at which students who had a probability of X of successfully answering the question. The probability X is set at 65 for free-response questions and 74 for multiple-choice questions.

The desired substantive interpretations of the achievement levels require the ability to give scores a justifiable criterion-referenced interpretation. Unfortunately, I do not think we are any closer to that goal now than we were when Forsyth (1991) concluded that the anchor points and NAEP proficiency scales did not "yield valid criterion-referenced interpretations" (p. 9). The goal continues to have appeal, but we are a long way from achieving it.

CONCLUSIONS

Cronbach (1988) remarked that validation "is a public spectacle combining the attractions of chess and mud wrestling" (p. 3). Although the validation work on the NAEP achievement levels does not make a particularly happy tale, it does illustrate Cronbach's point. The extended validity debates surrounding the achievement levels have resulted in some changes—changes, in my view, that have generally been in the right direction. These changes have generally been in the direction of restricting inferences or making more modest claims. The removal of the implicit, but unsupported, predictions from the achievement-level descriptions is one such example. The discontinuation of use of exemplar items that few students in an achievement-level interval could actually do or that many students at a lower level answered correctly is another.

More important, the experience illustrates the point that Messick (1995) made that the construct validity of the assessment and the standards cannot be separated. The constructs that NAEP is intended to measure are, as Millman (1994) said, broad and elusive. Perhaps it should be no surprise that strong criterion-reference interpretations cannot be supported for such constructs. In any event, the validity evidence provides a strong basis for arguing for more modest inferences and interpretations of achievement levels. As Glass (1978) suggested almost two decades ago, we can agree that increasing scores over time, whether in the form of percentage at or above arbitrary cutscores or changes in other statistics such as means or the location of various percentile ranks on the scale, is desirable. Maybe we would be better off reducing further the surplus meaning associated with achievement levels and focusing attention on changes in performance measured against constant scale points, however they are labeled.

ACKNOWLEDGMENTS

This article was commissioned by the Committee on the Evaluation of National and State Assessments of Educational Progress for the NAEP Achievement Levels: Setting Consensus Goals for Academic Achievement workshop, Washington, DC,

December 1996. This article was not reviewed by the Committee or the National Research Council, so the views expressed are solely my own.

REFERENCES

Augustus F. Hawkins–Robert T. Stafford Elementary and Secondary School Improvement Amendments, Pub. L. 100–297, Part C, § 3403(6)(A) (1988).
American College Testing Program. (1993). *Setting achievement levels on the 1992 National Assessment of Educational Progress in mathematics, reading and writing: A technical report on reliability and validity*. Iowa City, IA: Author.
American Educational Research Association, American Psychological Association, and the National Council on Measurement in Education. (1985). *Standards for educational and psychological testing*. Washington, DC: American Psychological Association.
Beatty, A. S., Reese, C. M., Persky, H. R., & Carr, P. (1996). *NAEP 1994 U.S. history report card: Findings from the National Assessment of Educational Progress*. Washington, DC: National Center for Education Statistics.
Berk, R. A. (1995). Standard-setting—The next generation. *Proceedings of the joint conference on standard setting for large-scale assessments of the National Assessment Governing Board (NAGB) and the National Center for Education Statistics (NCES)* (Vol. 2, pp. 161–181). Washington, DC: National Assessment Governing Board and National Center for Education Statistics.
Brennan, R. L. (1995). Standard setting from the perspective of generalizability theory. *Proceedings of the joint conference on Standard Setting for Large-Scale Assessments of the National Assessment Governing Board (NAGB) and the National Center for Education Statistics (NCES)* (Vol. 2, pp. 269–287). Washington, DC: National Assessment Governing Board and National Center for Education Statistics.
Burstein, L., Koretz, D. M., Linn, R. L., Baker, E. L., Sugrue, B., Novak, J., & Lewis, E. (1995–96). Describing performance standards: The validity of the 1992 NAEP achievement level descriptors as characterizations of mathematics performance. *Educational Assessment, 3*, 9–51.
Burstein, L., Koretz, D. M., Linn, R. L., Sugrue, B., Novak, J., Lewis, E., & Baker, E. L. (1993, August). *The validity of interpretations of the 1992 NAEP achievement levels in mathematics* (Tech. Rep.). Los Angeles: University of California, Center for the Study of Evaluation.
Campbell, J. R., Donahue, P. L., Reese, C. M., & Phillips, G. W. (1996). *NAEP 1994 reading report card for the nation and the states: Findings from the National Assessment of Educational Progress and trial state assessment*. Washington, DC: National Center for Education Statistics.
Cizek, G. J. (1993). *Reactions to National Academy of Education report: Setting performance standards for student achievement*. Washington, DC: National Assessment Governing Board.
Cronbach, L. J. (1980). Validity on parole: How can we go straight? In W. B. Schrader (Ed.), *Proceedings of the 1979 ETS invitational conference. New directions for testing and assessment: Measuring progress over a decade* (pp. 99–108). San Francisco: Jossey-Bass.
Cronbach, L. J. (1988). Five perspectives on validity argument. In H. Wainer & H. I. Braun (Eds.), *Test validity* (pp. 3–17). Hillsdale, NJ: Lawrence Erlbaum Associates, Inc.
Cronbach, L. J. (1989). Construct validity after thirty years. In R. L. Linn (Ed.), *Proceedings of a symposium in honor of Lloyd G. Humphreys. Intelligence: Measurement theory and public policy* (pp. 147–171). Urbana, IL: University of Illinois Press.
Forsyth, R. A. (1991). Do NAEP scales yield valid criterion-referenced interpretations? *Educational Measurement: Issues and Practice, 10*(3), 3–9, 16.
Gipps, C. V. (1994). *Beyond testing: Towards a theory of educational assessment*. London: Falmer.

Glaser, R. (1963). Instructional technology and the measurement of learning outcomes: Some questions. *American Psychologist, 18,* 519–521.

Glaser, R., Linn, R., & Bohrnstedt, G. (1996). *Quality and utility: The 1994 trial state assessment in reading: The fourth report of the National Academy of Education Panel on the evaluation of the NAEP trial state assessment in reading.* Stanford, CA: Stanford University, National Academy of Education.

Glass, G. V. (1978). Standards and criteria. *Journal of Educational Measurement, 15,* 237–261.

Kane, M. T. (1992). An argument-based approach to validity. *Psychological Bulletin, 112,* 527–535.

Kane, M. T. (1993). *Comments on the NAE evaluation of the NAGB achievement levels.* Washington, DC: National Assessment Governing Board.

Kane, M. T. (1995). Examinee-centered versus task-centered standard setting. In *Proceedings of the joint conference on standard setting for large-scale assessments of the National Assessment Governing Board (NAGB) and the National Center for Education Statistics (NCES)* (Vol. 2, pp. 119–141). Washington, DC: National Assessment Governing Board and National Center for Education Statistics.

Koretz, D., & Deibert, E. (1995–96). Setting standards and interpreting achievement: A cautionary tale from the National Assessment of Educational Progress. *Educational Assessment, 3,* 53–81.

Linn, R. L., Koretz, D. M., Baker, E. L., & Burstein, L. (1991). *The validity and credibility of the achievement levels for the 1990 National Assessment of Educational Progress in mathematics.* (Tech. Report). Los Angeles: University of California, Center for the Study of Evaluation.

Lissitz, R. W., & Bourque, M. L. (1995). Reporting NAEP results using standards. *Educational Measurement: Issues and Practice, 14*(2), 14–23, 31.

Mehrens, W. A. (1995). Methodological issues in standard setting for educational exams. In *Proceedings of the joint conference on standard setting for large-scale assessments of the National Assessment Governing Board (NAGB) and the National Center for Education Statistics (NCES)* (Vol. 2, pp. 221–263). Washington, DC: National Assessment Governing Board and National Center for Education Statistics.

Messick, S. (1989). Validity. In R. L. Linn (Ed.), *Educational measurement* (3rd ed., pp. 13–103). New York: Macmillan.

Messick, S. (1995). Standards-based score interpretation: Establishing valid grounds for valid inferences. In *Proceedings of the joint conference on standard setting for large-scale assessments of the National Assessment Governing Board (NAGB) and the National Center for Education Statistics (NCES)* (Vol. II, pp. 291–305). Washington, DC: National Assessment Governing Board and National Center for Education Statistics.

Millman, J. (1994). Criterion-referenced testing 30 years later: Promise broken, promise kept. *Educational Measurement: Issues and Practice, 13*(4), 1–20, 39.

Mullis, I. V. A., Dossey, J. A., Owen, E. H., & Phillips, G. W. (1991). *The state of mathematics achievement: NAEP's 1990 assessment of the nation and the trial assessment of the states* (Rep. No. 21-ST-04). Washington, DC: National Center for Education Statistics.

Mullis, I. V. A., Dossey, J. A., Owen, E. H., & Phillips, G. W. (1993). *NAEP 1992 mathematics report card for the nation and the states: Data from the national and trial state assessments* (Rep. No. 23-ST-02). Washington, DC: National Center for Education Statistics.

Mullis, I. V. A., Owen, E. H., & Phillips, G. W. (1990). *America's challenge: Accelerating academic achievement: A summary of findings from 20 years of NAEP.* Princeton, NJ: Educational Testing Service.

National Assessment Governing Board. (1991). *Request for proposal: Statement of work for setting achievement levels on the 1992 National Assessment of Educational Progress in mathematics, reading, and writing.* Washington, DC: Author.

National Assessment Governing Board and National Center for Education Statistics. (1995). In *Proceedings of the Joint Conference on Standard Setting for Large-Scale Assessments of the*

National Assessment Governing Board (NAGB) and the National Center for Education Statistics (NCES) (Vol. II, pp. 143–160). Washington, DC: Author.

National Council of Teachers of Mathematics. (1989). *Curriculum and evaluation standards for school mathematics.* Reston, VA: Author.

National Education Goals Panel. (1995). *The national education goals report: Building a nation of learners, 1995.* Washington, DC: Author.

Persky, H. R., Reese, C. M., O'Sullivan, C. Y., Lazer, S., Moore, J., & Shakrani, S. (1996). *NAEP 1994 geography report card: Findings from the National Assessment of Educational Progress.* Washington, DC: National Center for Education Statistics.

Shanker, A. (1990). The end of the traditional model of schooling and a proposal for using incentives to restructure schools. *Phi Delta Kappan, 71,* 344–348.

Shepard, L. A. (1993). Evaluating test validity. *Review of Research in Education, 19,* 405–450.

Shepard, L. A. (1995). Implications for standard setting of the National Academy of Education evaluation of the National Assessment of Educational Progress achievement levels. In *Proceedings of the joint conference on standard setting for large-scale assessments of the National Assessment Governing Board (NAGB) and the National Center for Education Statistics (NCES)* (Vol. 2, pp. 143–160). Washington, DC: National Assessment Governing Board and National Center for Education Statistics.

Shepard, L. A., Glaser, R., Linn, R. L., & Bohrnstedt, G. (1993). *Setting performance standards for student achievement: A report of the National Academy of Education Panel of the evaluation of the NAEP trial state assessment: An evaluation of the 1992 achievement levels.* Stanford, CA: Stanford University, National Academy of Education.

Stufflebeam, D., Jaeger, R. M., & Scriven, M. (1991, August). *Summative evaluation of the National Assessment Governing Board's inaugural 1990–91 effort to set achievement levels on the National Assessment of Educational Progress.* Washington, DC: National Assessment Governing Board.

U.S. Department of Education. (1997). *A call to action for American education in the 21st century.* Washington, DC: Author.

U.S. General Accounting Office. (1993). *Educational achievement standards: NAGB's approach yields misleading interpretations* (Rep. No. GAO–PEMD–93–12). Washington, DC: Author.

Zieky, M. J. (1995). A historical perspective on setting standards. *Proceedings of the joint conference on standard setting for large-scale assessments of the National Assessment Governing Board (NAGB) and the National Center for Education Statistics (NCES)* (Vol. 2, pp. 1–38). Washington, DC: National Assessment Governing Board and National Center for Education Statistics.

Implications of Market-Basket Reporting for Achievement-Level Setting

Robert J. Mislevy
Educational Testing Service
Princeton, New Jersey

In this article, I discuss ways in which reporting National Assessment of Educational Progress (NAEP) results in terms of a market basket of tasks would affect achievement-level reporting. After reviewing current NAEP reporting and achievement-level setting procedures, 3 market-basket variations are described. Ways in which achievement-level standards would be set, interpreted, and validated are then discussed. The conclusions are as follows: (a) the structure of the market-basket reporting scale can be exploited to simplify a key step in the standard-setting process, namely mapping item- or booklet-level judgments to the reporting scale; (b) the more transparent meaning of market-basket scores, in contrast to scaled scores and behavioral descriptions, clarifies the limitations of NAEP performances as evidence about the range of student proficiencies and accomplishments that the public's and educators' interests may span; and (c) market-basket reporting approaches that enable individual students to take a full market-basket set of items simplify data-gathering and analysis for validity studies of achievement-level set-points and interpretations.

In this article, I discuss how summarizing National Assessment of Educational Progress (NAEP) results in terms of a market basket of items would affect achievement-level reporting. After a review of current NAEP reporting and achievement-level setting (ALS) practices, market-basket reporting is described. Discussion then turns to the mechanics of standard-setting procedures and to validity studies meant to ground ALS procedures and inferences.

Requests for reprints should be sent to Robert J. Mislevy, Educational Testing Service, Princeton, NJ 08541.

NAEP SCALING AND ALS PROCEDURES

NAEP Administration and Scaling Procedures

NAEP is a large-scale, nationally representative, cross-sectional survey. It is timed, standardized, and, from the students', teachers', and school administrators' points of view, low-stakes. It is not directly connected with students' instruction, in that the tasks they are administered have not been selected in light of what they have been working on in their classes, and students receive no feedback on how they have done. Assessments are carried out at Grades 4, 8, and 12.

Developing the NAEP content framework is a national consensus process. Item specifications follow from the content framework in a subject area, and a large collection of tasks is assembled to administer to students. The tasks cover the content specified in the framework, and they span a range of formats and modes. The 1996 NAEP science assessment, for example, contained both multiple-choice items and open-ended tasks, which could appear independently, in a thematic block, or in the context of a hands-on experiment. The collection of tasks needed to span the content framework is far too large to administer to an individual student. Item sampling designs present subsets of items to students—about a single class period's worth—to maintain broad content coverage by the assessment as a whole without burdening individual students or schools. NAEP uses item response theory (IRT) to integrate information from overlapping booklets of tasks, producing summary distributions of population and subpopulation performance on a 0 to 500 scale.

IRT posits an unobservable proficiency variable, say θ, to account for a student's performance on the tasks in a scaling area, which may be all tasks in the subject area, or a subarea such as algebra or numbers and operations in mathematics. Fitting the IRT model across test booklets means estimating the relation between θ and the probabilities of responses to individual tasks—right or wrong for multiple-choice items, ordered score categories on open-ended tasks. These relations are expressed by item parameters for each of the tasks and their potential responses, which are combined with θ through the IRT model. One can (a) draw inferences about θ from responses to any subset of tasks and (b) project, given a value of θ, likely performance on any subset of tasks—single items, specified collections, or the entire scaling-area pool.

Present purposes do not require the details of IRT, but one feature is pertinent: Item parameters are strongly linked to the empirical difficulties of items, that is, the proportions of students who respond correctly on right–wrong tasks, or score at successive levels on ordered-category open-ended tasks. For example, a student is modeled as being more likely to correctly answer a right–wrong task with an easy parameter than one with a hard item parameter. The following discussion will simplify NAEP procedures to highlight the implications of this fact. I will speak of an item's difficulty parameter as if it were the only parameter involved; in practice, other item parameters moderate its effect. I will also discuss ALS as it concerns a single scaling area. In practice, subject areas comprising multiple subscales are reported in terms of an average over subscales, which also moderates the relation between item difficulty parameters and empirical difficulties.

NAEP ALS Procedures

Since its inception, NAEP has reported how students do on the tasks they are administered, or what they actually do in the NAEP setting. Since the early 1990s, under the direction of the National Assessment Governing Board (NAGB), NAEP has incorporated reports that place these results in the context of what students should be able to do—that is, in terms of performance standards. Three levels are specified at each grade—basic, proficient, and advanced. Each level is defined by a particular point on the NAEP scale. Results reported in terms of performance standards include statements such as "35% of the fourth-grade students are at or above the basic level," meaning that 35% of the estimated fourth grade distribution on the reporting scale lies above the basic cutpoint. Table 1 shows the estimated proportions of students at or above the NAEP achievement-level cutpoints in the 1992 mathematics assessment, as expressed on the 0 to 500 reporting scale.

This manner of calculating proportions of students at or above performance levels implies that what students actually do across a range of tasks and what they should do can be summarized on the same one-dimensional scale, be it the IRT-based scales discussed later or the market-basket scales defined in the next section. I shall later discuss how this simple comparison can mask more complex discrepancies between actual and desired performance.

Although NAEP ALS procedures continue to evolve, the following discussion based on the 1992 reading assessment (Bourque, 1995; also see American College

TABLE 1
1992 NAEP Mathematics Assessment Results in Terms of Scale Scores

Grade	Average	Advanced		Proficient		Basic	
		Cutpoint	% At or Above	Cutpoint	% At or Above	Cutpoint	% At or Above
4	220	282	3.1	249	19.1	214	61.5
8	268	333	3.8	299	23.6	262	55.6
12	300	367	2.8	336	14.9	288	63.1

Note. NAEP = National Assessment of Educational Progress.

Testing [ACT], 1995) reflects the key steps in the process. For each grade level, a panel is selected from across the country and across walks of life. In light of background information, the panelists first create summary verbal descriptions of the performances that basic, proficient, and advanced students at a given grade level would exhibit. Then, task by task, panelists make judgments that constitute the basic data for determining cutpoints. For multiple-choice and short open-ended tasks, they indicate the probability of success of marginally basic, proficient, and advanced students. For extended constructed-response tasks, they select from a representative sample three performances that they feel represent marginal performance at each level. They are given feedback about empirical results for student performance, other panelists' ratings, and the levels on the reporting scale that their item-by-item judgments imply.

A critical step is translating item-by-item judgments to the score scale. The IRT item parameters that link patterns of student performance to θ are now also used to map panelists' ratings to θ. Suppose just one item, say Item J, were involved. If a panelist feels that 60% of the students who just qualify as basic would respond correctly to Item J, then the θ value that would lead to 60% probability of a correct response through the IRT model is this item-judgment's contribution, from this panelist, to defining the basic cutpoint.

However, each panelist rates many items, and each such rating implies a cutpoint on the IRT scale to define basic performance as particular to that item. Separate averages of a panelist's item-by-item implied basic cutpoints are calculated for extended constructed response items and for multiple-choice and short constructed response items. These two averages are averaged together in turn, using information weights from the IRT model (which bear no necessary relation to the importance weights that a panelist may impose).

Rater Inconsistency in IRT Standard Setting

If a panelist's ratings fall in the same order as empirical results for the same items, the IRT mappings of her ratings point to similar item-by-item cutpoint values of θ. If her ratings differ in order from empirical difficulties, however, they point to different values of θ. Perhaps the panelist felt that the levels of performance she would demand to rate a student proficient were surpassed by most current students on multiple-choice items, but only a few students exhibited the levels of performance she would demand for proficient performance on extended-constructed response tasks. Her judgments for these latter tasks would point to a higher level of θ for the proficient cutoff than her ratings for multiple-choice items. This phenomenon is referred to as *rater inconsistency* in the standard-setting literature, implicitly pointing an accusing finger at the rater.

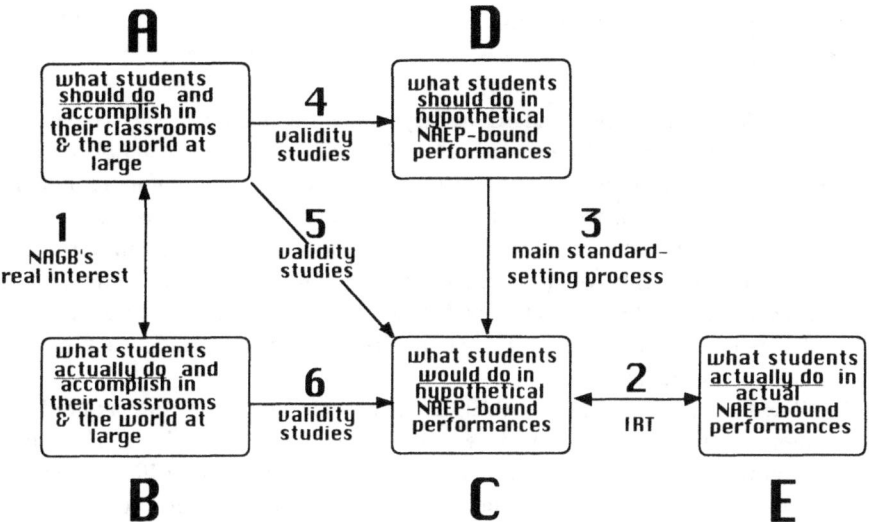

FIGURE 1 Some relations in achievement-level reporting. NAGB = National Assessment Governing Board; NAEP = National Assessment of Educational Progress.

However, the only inconsistency may lie between the patterns in the judge's relative standards across items and the patterns in items' relative empirical percentages-correct at a particular point in time, the latter determined largely by existing curricula and instructional practice. There is no logical necessity for these orderings to agree, and it need not signal problems with the judge's ratings if they do not. Discrepancies arise from different emphases in actual and desired curricula. Mapped to the IRT scale, consistently different cutpoints may be found for tasks distinguished by type or topic, and reliably different proportions of students can be proficient in each. Aggregate cutpoints depend on the number of the various kinds of tasks and on items' information values from the IRT model—a projection that need not reflect panelists' views on the desired levels and relative importance of performance on the various subsets of tasks. A disadvantage of summarizing many item-level judgments as a single point on a unidimensional scale, then, is that it is not always possible to capture valid opinions about differences between what is and what ought to be in a single common scale.

Some Important Relations in Achievement-Level Reporting

Figure 1 depicts some important relations in setting, interpreting, and validating standards in NAEP. It will serve as the basis of further discussions in the Market-

Basket Reporting and ALS section and the ALS Validity Studies Under Market-Basket Reporting section. These are the important points so far:

- Box A represents the standards as they are summarized in the verbal descriptions: What students at a given grade should be able to do and accomplish in the subject area—not just on NAEP tasks and in the NAEP setting, but more broadly. Perceptions of basic, proficient, and advanced students, as construed in everyday parlance, encompass this broad scope of relevant knowledge and accomplishment.
- Box B represents what students actually can do and accomplish, again construed more broadly than can be evidenced by their performance in NAEP alone. It is the A–B comparison (Link 1) that NAGB would be most interested in, were the evidence available.
- Box E represents the raw NAEP data: students' right or wrong and ordered responses, omits, and not-reached items in the many NAEP booklets. These data are currently integrated into a single IRT scale (or a composite of IRT subscales), a summary that can be projected to performance in the collection of tasks as a whole, or Box C; this is Link 2 in Figure 1.
- Box C represents the data summaries that standard NAEP data collection efforts provide: Distributions of students' performance in terms of the scale of 0 to 500 NAEP θ scale, reflecting results confined to NAEP data tasks and administration conditions. Box C is a proxy for Box B. In some respects it fails to capture aspects of learning that we as a society desire of our students because it does not gauge their performance in long-term projects, self-selected work, collaborations with others, or situations in which external resources are used. This is *construct underrepresentation,* to use Messick's (1989) term. Moreover, the specific circumstances and formats under which NAEP data are collected will influence students' motivation and opportunity to perform. These factors affect performance, even though we would prefer that they did not. In Messick's terms, this is *construct irrelevant variance.*
- Box D represents judgments about levels of performance in NAEP performance: What levels of performance on the idealized NAEP scale (Box C) should demarcate basic, proficient, and advanced performance in the subject area for the grade in question? It is this C–D link (Link 3) that current ALS procedures address.

How do we know whether considering students advanced on the basis of their NAEP performance matches what we would conclude if we observed them over time, in and out of their classrooms? The answer is validity studies—to explore the relation between NAEP performance and achievement levels with respect to what is captured, what is missed, how students who do well in school perform on NAEP, how students deemed advanced on NAEP do in school, and so on. Validity studies use information beyond standard NAEP data to investigate the implications of ALS procedures. The ALS Validity Studies Under Market-Basket Reporting section addresses the various kinds of validity studies that Links 4, 5, and 6 represent.

MARKET-BASKET REPORTING: DEFINITIONS AND VARIATIONS

A market basket is a specific collection of items that one may administer, scores on which constitutes a reporting scale. This could be performance in terms of true scores or observed scores, as discussed by Forsyth, Hambleton, Linn, Mislevy, and Yen (1996); the following discussion will focus on the simpler route of observed scores. Both right–wrong items and open-ended items can be included, once well-defined scoring rules are agreed on. In terms of Figure 1, market-basket reporting replaces the scale of 0 to 500 IRT-based θ scale with a scale based on (actual or potentially) observable scores for market-basket collections of tasks.

The number and mix of items in a market basket can be determined by consensus, subject to the following considerations:

- *Representativeness:* A range of item types and content is desirable, as are illustrations of key skills and concepts. Experimental and specialized tasks may appear in nonmarket-basket assessment forms.
- *Replicability:* Unlike the Bureau of Labor Statistics' Consumer Price Index, which maintains a fixed collection of consumer products for a period of years, it may be desirable to be able to construct multiple parallel market baskets so that one or more can be released after being used, while the rest remain secure for use in subsequent assessment years.
- *Size:* Three possible sizes of market baskets are discussed next, their comparative advantages and disadvantages highlighted. The variations are (a) a typical booklet that an actual student can take; (b) a somewhat longer, but not exhaustive, collection of actual items; and (c) a large collection that effectively defines the subject domain of interest.

The items in a market basket would be made public to give users a concrete reference for score levels. Differences between Boxes B and C in Figure 1 would become apparent. The evidentiary grounding for a statement such as "35% of the fourth-grade students are at or above the basic level" would become clear; 35% of the students would get scores of at least X_B, the cutscore for basic performance on a set of items that everyone can see, examine, or even try themselves. Moreover, what is not in the market basket also becomes clear—skills and accomplishments, such as long-term projects or success at learning specific things they have studied, that are not tapped in standard NAEP data collection efforts.

Variation 1: Market Basket—The Size of a Typical Test Form

In this variation, a first market-basket collection would be used to establish a reporting metric—observed scores on this set of items, and other sets that are very much like it—and released to the public. Replicate market-basket collections would be administered in the same assessment and, having been built to be parallel to the original collection, could be linked to it with standard equating functions. Algorithms are available for constructing, say, two to six replicate market-basket collections from a suitable startup pool of items (e.g., Stocking et al., 1991). Other booklets could be included in an assessment without the tight constraints required for market-basket forms. Information from these forms could be reported in its own right, or projected to the market-basket scale by using more complex IRT procedures.

An advantage to having market-basket collections that could be released (and replaced) over time is that these collections and their relation to the reporting metric could be made available to embed in other projects—state or local assessments, national or international surveys, program evaluations, and public and private research projects. With the observed-score metric of the market basket as the reporting scale, a project could get observed score distributions on the NAEP scale without complex statistical methods. As discussed in the ALS Validity Studies Under Market-Basket Reporting section, this advantage facilitates validity studies of achievement-level cutpoints.

Variation 2: Market Basket Larger Than a Typical Form

A disadvantage of Variation 1 is that the breadth of the subject domain could probably not be fully represented with a set of items that a student would be administered in a testing session. Multiple one-period collections of tasks may together adequately convey the mix of formats, skills, and topics specified in the content framework. This larger collection could serve as a market basket for reporting results. The resulting advantages would be better representativeness and communication of content coverage. The disadvantage is that observed scores on a typical administered booklet no longer provide unbiased estimates of population distributions other than central tendency—in particular, not proportions of students at or above proficiency level cutpoints. More complex statistical procedures would be required for such inferences in terms of these larger market baskets.

Variation 3: Market Basket Equals Subject Domain

Darrell Bock's (1996) domain-referenced scoring marshaled a sufficient number of items to constitute an operational definition of skill in that domain, and reports results in terms of an expected score on the collection as a whole that could be anywhere from 500 to 5,000 items. To accomplish this virtually requires establishing IRT or similar models for the items in the domain. Because no student would ever be able to take the entire item pool, scaling models would be the vehicle through which predictive distributions on the domain as a whole were calculated. Bock envisages releasing the entire domain of items immediately to the public to stimulate discussion and learning in the subject area.

MARKET-BASKET REPORTING AND ALS

In this section, I address the nuts and bolts of standard setting under a system of market-basket reporting, or Links 2 and 3 in Figure 1. The ALS Validity Studies Under Market-Basket Reporting section will address the broader questions of validity, or Links 4, 5, and 6.

Impact on the Mechanics of Standard Setting

Link 2 represents the mapping to the reporting scale; from actual students' performances in whatever booklets they have been administered. The current system uses IRT to project from task performances to the subject area scale of 0 to 500 reporting scale. Under market-basket reporting, performances are mapped to score distributions on a specified collection of tasks. The mapping function is an equating function if the student has responded to a replicate market-basket form under in Variation 1 (see the subsection on Market Basket the Size of a Typical Test Form), or an IRT-based mapping not unlike that of the current system under the other market-basket variations or under Variation 1 from nonmarket-basket booklets. The more important difference between market-basket reporting and the current system lies with Link 3, or ALS: Under market-basket reporting, the IRT mapping associated with Link 2 is not required for achievement level setting.

The current NAEP ALS procedures' reliance on item-by-item judgments to define cutpoints has been subject to considerable scrutiny (e.g., National Academy of Education, 1993). The sum of apparently reasonable but uncertain item-level judgments need not necessarily reflect a panelist's judgment about overall performance on, say, a given assessment booklet. It has been suggested that item-by-item judgments be supplemented by judgments based on entire booklets, calling for basic, proficient, and advanced cutpoints with respect to performance on the booklet as a whole. Under the current system, such judgments can be carried out, and the IRT models can be used to translate those judgments into points on the θ scale (for an illustration, see ACT, 1995).

With market-basket reporting, judgments in terms of performance on the market-basket collections of tasks suggest themselves as the natural mechanism for standard setting. Judgments about cutpoints for overall performance on market-basket collections of items are either on the reporting scale immediately or removed by just a simple, previously calculated, equating function. IRT procedures can be eliminated from the ALS process entirely, thereby removing steps that are complex, unfamiliar to the lay panelists, data dependent, and possibly inappropriate for summarizing panelists' item-by-item judgments onto the reporting scale in the first place (see the Rater Inconsistency in IRT Standard Setting subsection).

Panelists may still work through a market-basket collection of tasks one by one, setting expectations for proficient performance, and then find that actual students who perform at that level typically exceed their expectations for some subsets of items (e.g., multiple choice) but fall short on others (e.g., open ended). Their frustration in an ability to express the *patterns* as well as the overall *level* of proficiency that they have in mind does not reflect a shortcoming of ALS under market-basket reporting per se. It reflects, rather, the constraint of having to collapse both judgments and empirical performances to a single scale that cannot capture pattern differences. One solution may be separate standards for different subdomains of tasks. Another is summary reporting on the domain as a whole, supplemented by in-depth discussions of profile differences when they exist.

Market-Basket ALS Reports

Table 1 shows achievement-level scale of 0 to 500 θ scale cutpoints and proportions of students above those cutpoints in the 1992 NAEP mathematics assessment. Using data from this assessment, Johnson (1996) illustrated Variation 1 of the market-basket approach. He created a mock market basket for each grade by selecting three released assessment blocks[1] from that grade that together best reflected the content framework. The blocks that constituted these market baskets never appeared together in the operational data collection, so estimated distributions of market-basket scores were calculated through the IRT models.[2]

Cutpoints for basic, proficient, and advanced performance on the market basket were determined as those scores on a grade's market basket that gave the same proportions of the population above the cutpoints obtained in the actual ALS procedures. Table 2 shows the resulting cutpoints and proportions of students above them—the latter figures identical to those of Table 1 by construction.

An examination of Table 2 shows that basic cutpoint scores were similar across grades, as were proficient and advanced cutpoint scores. This was largely coinci-

---

[1] Blocks are independently constructed and separately timed sets of items, three of which constitute the cognitive portion of a student's NAEP booklet.

[2] Files of NAEP "plausible values" (which had been constructed to reflect distributions of performance across the NAEP mathematics subscales in each of the three grades) were used to generate, through the IRT models and item parameters, draws of item responses to the market-basket tasks. Market-basket scores were sums of these.

TABLE 2
1992 NAEP Mathematics Assessment Results in Terms of Market Basket
(Percentage of Total Score)

Grade	Average	Advanced		Proficient		Basic	
		Cutpoint	% At or Above	Cutpoint	% At or Above	Cutpoint	% At or Above
4	41	80	3.1	58	19.1	34	61.5
8	42	73	3.8	55	23.6	37	55.6
12	40	75	2.8	57	14.9	33	63.1

Note. NAEP = National Assessment of Educational Progress.

dental because there is no reason that the Grade 8 market-basket tasks would be relatively harder or easier for 8th-grade students than the Grade 12 tasks were for 12th-grade students. It could have happened, for example, that a score of 70% on the Grade 8 market basket would represent proficient performance for 8th-grade students, but a score of only 60% on a distinct and coincidentally harder Grade 12 market basket would represent advanced performance for 12th-grade students. There is no necessary relation between cutpoints for different grades.

ALS VALIDITY STUDIES UNDER MARKET-BASKET REPORTING

For examining the validity of the achievement-level results, market-basket reporting can facilitate aspects of construct analysis and simplify studies using external data.

Role of the Market Basket in ALS Construct Analysis

By making manifest the referent of both observed performance and cutpoint scores, market-basket reporting facilitates analyses of construct representation and the problems that it can cause in standard setting. NAEP results can only reflect information from the tasks actually administered, whether results are reported on a θ scale or a market-basket scale—but it is harder to ignore this when the market-basket tasks are in plain sight. Tasks fade into the background when discussions revolve around mathematics proficiency in the abstract, and one may forget about the aspects of mathematics proficiency that standard NAEP data cannot capture.

Consider a basketball analogy. Shooting free throws is an important part of basketball proficiency but far from the only part. What happens if we gather only free throw data from basketball players, and we try to set a standard for National Basketball Association (NBA)-level proficiency? Suppose we can get excellent data for free throw shooting (Box C)—which is, however, only part of basketball proficiency (Box B).

Now the average free throw shooting percentage in the NBA is about 70%. Should we say that 70% is the cutpoint for NBA-caliber performance on free throw shooting? If it is, far more players will exceed this standard than can actually play NBA-level basketball. Suppose that only 0.01% of the basketball player population can play at the NBA level. Should we set our free throw cutpoint high enough that only this many players exceed it—perhaps only those making 95% of their free throws? We would have matched the proportion of the population who can shoot free throws this well with the proportion who can play at the NBA level. The problem is that they are not the same players! The *Guinness Book of World Records* (Young, 1997) says that Thomas Amberry sunk 2,750 consecutive free throws in November 1993, but this does not make him a great basketball player. Shaquille O'Neal makes only about 50% of his free throws—yet in 1995 the NBA named him one of the 50 greatest NBA players of all time (Vancil, 1996)!

Appropriate use of free throws as a measure of basketball proficiency takes construct underrepresentation into account. We may say that 70% is the cutoff for NBA-level performance but realize that this aspect of performance alone does not make an NBA player. We can track changes in performance over time, and we can compare groups—but we know that for a complete picture, we would need to collect more data about basketball proficiency.

Role of the Market Basket in ALS Empirical Analyses

Empirical studies of the validity of achievement-level reporting examine results associated with the scale and the cutpoints. It is straightforward to gather and interpret data in supplemental studies under Variations 1 and 2 of market-basket reporting because performance on market-basket collections of tasks arrives on the reporting and standard-setting scale. Under Variation 1, students can be tested under conditions close to operational data collection. Under Variation 2, extended testing sessions are required, but actual market-basket observed scores can be obtained.

Various kinds of validity studies correspond to Links 4, 5, and 6. Any of these studies could be carried out with θ scale reporting; the difference is merely one of convenience in gathering and analyzing the resulting data. Johnson, Liang, Norris, and Nicewander (1996), for example, described a validity study for U.S. history and geography standards in which a double-length NAEP assessment—which could serve as a Variation 2 market basket—is administered to students in the classes of teachers who participated in the standard setting process. Analysis is always complex under current IRT-based reporting procedures because IRT and marginal estimation procedures are required to bridge Link 2. If a market-basket collection of tasks is administered under market-basket reporting procedures, Link 2 is immediate.

Link 6 corresponds to collecting different kinds of performance data in different contexts, along with performance on market-basket tasks, and then mapping out the relations among them. Market-basket performance data can be collected along with grades, extended project ratings, teachers' evaluations, or standardized achievement test results. A fuller picture emerges of what performance on the market basket does and does not capture (construct representativeness), and the levels of market-basket performance that go along with levels of performance on other aspects of students' skills. An ACT (1995) validity study found that teachers' own conceptions of proficient performance in the classroom included factors such as motivation and maturity that are not addressed by NAEP performance.

Link 5 is similar to the basketball example discussed earlier, if we were to examine free-throw performance of NBA players and college players. Students determined by other sources of evidence as either meeting or failing to meet a given standard are administered the market basket of tasks. Link 5 corresponds to examining the performance of the groups, to learn, for example, what levels of performance they exhibit on the market-basket scale, and to determine the extent to which performance on the market-basket tasks differentiates students judged as meeting or not meeting a standard.

Link 4 carries the analysis begun with Link 5 a step farther. It corresponds to using the comparison of the market-basket score distributions as a source of information about what the cutoff points should be. Consider, as an example, a group of Grade 12 students taking Advanced Placement (AP) Mathematics. Those who pass (i.e., attain a score of 3 or higher on the AP test) may be considered advanced, whereas those who have taken the course but not passed may be considered only proficient. Assuming that the market-basket scores of the passers tend to be higher than those of nonpassers, the point at which their distributions cross is one reasonable suggestion for the location of the advanced cutpoint (Figure 2).

CONCLUSIONS

Market-basket reporting has been suggested as a means of reporting NAEP results that will help the public and policy makers relate those results to actual student behavior. In this article, I have examined the impact of market-basket reporting on setting, interpreting, and validating achievement levels. These are my conclusions:

1. The structure of the market-basket reporting scale can be exploited to simplify a key step in the standard-setting process, namely, mapping item- or booklet-level judgments to the reporting scale.

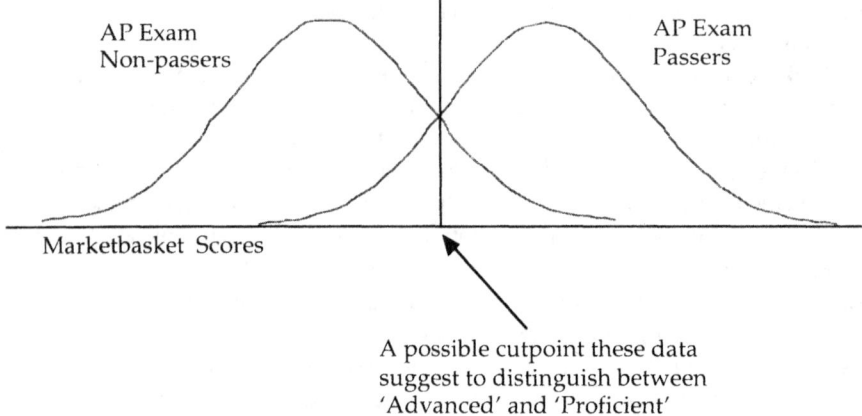

FIGURE 2 Hypothetical market-basket score distributions of Grade 12 students who did and did not pass an Advanced Placement (AP) Mathematics examination.

2. The more transparent meaning of market-basket scores, in contrast to scaled scores and behavioral descriptions, clarifies the limitations of NAEP performances as evidence about the range of student proficiencies and accomplishments that the public's and educators' interests may span.

3. Market-basket reporting approaches that enable individual students to take a full market-basket set of items simplify data gathering and analysis for validity studies of achievement-level set points and interpretations.

The limitations noted in 2 are not caused by market-basket reporting but rather exposed under market-basket reporting. They are inherent limitations in the evidence that NAEP data provide for various inferences. It is easy to lose sight of these limitations when complex analyses are involved and to extend interpretations beyond those the data support. As Kin Hubbard reminded us, "T'ain't what a man don't know that hurts him. It's what he knows that just ain't so" (as cited in Peters, 1997, p. 258).

ACKNOWLEDGMENTS

The material in this article was presented at the Committee on the Evaluation of National and State Assessments of Educational Progress for the National Assessment in Educational Progress Achievement Levels: Setting Consensus Goals for Academic Achievement workshop on December 1996 in Washington, DC under the auspices of the National Research Council's Board on Testing and Assessment. The views expressed here are solely my own. The descriptions of market-basket reporting approaches and Figure 1 are extensions of my contributions to the Design–Feasibility Team report to the National Assessment Governing Board. I am grateful to Jim Carlson and an anonymous reviewer for helpful comments, and to Gene Johnson for Tables 1 and 2, which were based on work supported under the National Assessment of Educational Progress (Cooperative Agreement R999C500001) as administered by the Office of Educational Research and Improvement, U.S. Department of Education.

REFERENCES

American College Testing. (1995). *Preliminary report on the 1994 NAEP achievement level setting process for U.S. history and geography.* Iowa City, IA: Author.

Bock, R. D. (1996). *Domain-referenced reporting in large-scale educational assessments.* Commissioned paper to the National Academy of Education for the Capstone Report of the NAE Technical Review Panel on State–NAEP Assessment, Washington, DC.

Bourque, M. L. (1995). Setting the NAEP achievement levels for the 1994 reading assessment. In J. Mazzeo, N. L. Allen, & D. L. Kline (Eds.), *Technical report of the 1994 trial state assessment program in reading* (Appendix F, pp. 341–371). Washington, DC: National Center for Education Statistics.

Forsyth, R., Hambleton, R., Linn, R., Mislevy, R., & Yen, W. (1996). *Design feasibility team report to the National Assessment Governing Board.* Washington, DC: National Assessment Governing Board.

Johnson, E. G. (1996, August). *A demonstration of market-basket reporting.* Paper presented at a meeting of the National Assessment Governing Board, Washington, DC.

Johnson, E. G., Liang, J.-L., Norris, N., & Nicewander, A. (1996, April). *Directly estimated NAEP scale scores from double-length assessment booklets—A replacement for plausible values?* Paper presented at the meeting of National Council of Measurement in Education, New York.

Messick, S. (1989). Validity. In R. L. Linn (Ed.), *Educational measurement* (3rd ed., pp. 13–103). New York: American Council on Education and Macmillan.

National Academy of Education. (1993). *Setting performance standards for student achievement.* Stanford, CA: Author.

Peter, L. J. (1977). *Peter's quotations: Ideas for our time.* New York: Bantam.

Stocking, M. L., Swanson, L., & Pearlman, M. (1991). *Automated item selection (AIS) methods in the ETS testing environment.* (Rep. No. 91–5). Princeton, NJ: Educational Testing Service.

Vancil, M. (1996). *The NBA at fifty.* New York: Park Lane.

Young, M. C. (1997). *The Guinness book of world records 1998* (37th ed.). New York: Penguin.

Setting Performance Standards for Professional Licensure and Certification

Barbara S. Plake
Oscar and Luella Buros Center for Testing
University of Nebraska

Credentialing programs were surveyed to ascertain the procedures that they use to set performance standards on multiple-choice and open-ended assessments. For multiple-choice assessments, these programs mostly employ variations on the Angoff (1971) standard-setting method. Procedures used with open-ended questions showed more divergence; some agencies use a question by question approach, whereas others utilize methods that consider the assessment results more holistically. Implications of these standard-setting practices from credentialing agencies to the National Assessment of Educational Progress (NAEP), including the consequences of the assessment on the individual candidate, the matrix sampling construction of NAEP assessments, the multiple cutpoints of the NAEP assessment program, and the types of validity evidence that are typically gathered to support the validity of the performance standard, are discussed. Generalizations of these standard-setting methods from the field of professional licensure and certification should be made with caution.

Decisions about who is qualified to perform professional functions linked to practice in the professions have been made for centuries. Today, many professional programs make these decisions with the aid of assessments. These assessments should be developed to provide evidence of the candidate's relevant knowledges, skills, and abilities appropriate for being a licensed or certified professional in the field. The level of performance sufficient to receive the license or certificate is typically determined by employing some type of standard-setting procedure. The

---

Requests for reprints should be sent to Barbara S. Plake, Oscar and Luella Buros Center for Testing, 135 Bancroft Hall, University of Nebraska, Lincoln, NE 68588-0348.

purposes of this article are to (a) highlight some of the existing methods employed in the field of licensure and certification to set performance standards and (b) discuss the applicability of these methods to the National Assessment of Educational Progress (NAEP) program. For a basic orientation to existing standard-setting methods, see Mills and Melican (1988).

In this article, two major distinctions are made: (a) methods that are used with multiple-choice items and (b) approaches involving use of open-ended (e.g., essays, oral examinations, simulated patient) questions. In each case, the current and prevalent standard-setting methods are identified.

Although there are important distinctions between licensure and certification programs, for the purposes of this article, these distinctions are not highlighted. Instead, the collective experience and wisdom of both licensure and certification fields are blended, with the primary focus being on the methods used for setting performance standards based on their assessments.

No attempt was made to survey all licensure and certification programs. Rather, the strategy used was to contact persons who have published in the field of setting of performance standards in licensure or certification fields or were known to be developing new methods. Therefore, there is no attempt to generalize the information contained in this article to the field of licensure and certification. Instead, in this article, I document what is being used or developed in several extant programs. However, there was an attempt to obtain some representation across disciplines. Licensure and certification programs in the fields of business (accountancy and financial analysis), computer technology (Novelle), professional education (National Board of Professional Teaching Standards), insurance, and allied health (optometry, poison control, radiological technicians, American Board of Internal Medicine, National Board of Medical Examiners, insurance, and the Board of Registry, representing fields of clinical pathology, technicians–technologists–pathologists, microbiology, blood banks, cytopathology, hermatology, clinical chemistry, and histotechnology). In addition, two professional consulting organizations whose clients include professional licensure and certification agencies were contacted: the Chauncey Group and Applied Measurement Professionals. In this article, discussions of standard-setting methods typically refer to generic disciplines, not the particular agencies. This strategy was employed because some of the agencies were reluctant to have their specific standard-setting approaches described in a public document due to concerns that their constituencies may use this information to influence candidate performance on the tests.

I end the article with a discussion of the new directions on the horizon for standard-setting methods for licensure and certification. Also, some considerations related to the utility of these approaches for standard-setting procedures for NAEP are presented.

CURRENT STANDARD-SETTING APPROACHES IN LICENSURE AND CERTIFICATION PROGRAMS

Multiple-Choice Questions

Consistent with the survey on national licensure examination programs conducted by Sireci and Biskin (1992), the most prevalent standard-setting method used with multiple-choice questions by the agencies contacted is the Angoff (1971) approach. Small variations on the traditional procedures (e.g., giving panelists categories for the item performance estimates for the minimally competent candidate [MCC], or providing candidate performance information) were common, but the basic strategy of convening a panel of experts, training them on the knowledge, skills, and abilities of the MCC, and having them make item performance estimates for such candidates was consistently followed. Some of the agencies put particular emphasis on certain aspects of the standard-setting procedure, either by focusing on the training of the experts or in running replications to study the stability and generalizability of the results. Also, some agencies made decisions about the acceptable amount of difference between the panelists' estimates of MCC item performance and actual candidate performance. For example, one agency employs a criterion of the minimal acceptable discrepancy between the judge's estimate of item performance and the actual candidate performance on that item (.20). If the differences exceed the minimum, optional strategies are used. These may entail discarding the item or modeling the relation between actual and predicted performance for the other items in the test and using the predicted value for the aberrant items.

As noted earlier, the implementation of the Angoff method varies somewhat in whether empirical data are provided and, if so, what data and when in the standard-setting session the data are provided. One program has elected not to use any performance data in the standard-setting process, contrary to conventional wisdom (Cizek, 1996) and prevalent practice (Jaeger, 1989; Mills, 1994). In communicating empirical information, most programs supply overall total candidate average item performance data. These data are provided after the panelists have made their initial round of item performance estimates. One program provides panelists with information on candidates' item performance by deciles on the total test score. This information is communicated in graphical form, showing the proportion of candidates within each decile band who correctly answered an item. These plots have the advantage of also communicating item discrimination information through the steepness of the adjacent histogram bars.

Some of the program personnel interviewed mentioned using adjustments to the final Angoff standard based on techniques described by de Gruijter (1985), Hofstee (1983), and Beuk (1984). The adjustments are based on the panelists' estimates of the overall score point that is appropriate for the cutscore and their anticipated proportion of candidates who will pass the examination. This information is often obtained by asking the panelists two sets of questions, such as the following:

1. Based on my review of this set of test items, I think that the percentage of correctly answered questions required to receive a passing grade should not go below ___% correct or above ___% correct. If I were to pick a single number as the requirement for passing, it would be ___% correct.

2. Based on my experience with this field of practice, I would not expect the overall failure rate for those making their first-time attempt at the examination to go below ___% fail or above ___% fail. If I were to select a single number as the expected failure rate for this group, it would be ___%.

Although analytic methods exist for adjusting ("compromising") the obtained standard with the information gathered from these questions, most of the agencies do not use information gained from these questions to make empirical adjustment (Fidler as cited in Browning, Bugbee, & Mullins, 1996). Instead, these questions were used to help in the training of panelists by (a) temporarily redirecting the judges' attention away from individual items and back to the overall test, prior to presenting them with empirical test data and (b) forcing the judges to formulate and express their ideas about the relation between the minimally acceptable performance levels and their expectations for the performance of a typical examinee group (Dillon, 1996; Dillon, Swanson, Nungester, Peskin, & Ross, 1993). This information can also be useful in identifying a panelist whose views about the acceptable minimal performance and pass rates are markedly different from that of the other panel members. This information could be used as a basis of discussion with the panelist or as the basis for deciding to diminish the impact of that panelist's views either by using the median, rather than the mean, as the summary statistic for calculating the final performance standard or by disregarding that panelist's data altogether. This information could also serve as a point of comparison between the panelists' overall perceptions and the results of their standard-setting efforts when communicating with the panelists between rounds in the Angoff standard-setting process.

Another issue to be considered when applying an Angoff standard-setting procedure is the qualifications of the expert panelists. Jaeger (1989, 1991) provided clear criteria for the qualifications of panelists for a judgmental standard-setting procedure. Among the criteria are expertise in the content area measured by the assessment. However, in some areas of licensure and certification, subspecialties are abundant, and even though the licensure and certification test is designed to provide a broad spectrum of expertise, panelists will vary in their degree of recent or relevant exposure to some of the content covered by the examinations. One program asks panelists to circle items in the test that they feel are outside their expertise. Item performance estimates on these circled items are then disregarded in the final computations.

Thus, some variations in the traditional Angoff procedures are being followed. However, these variations are viewed not as new or unique applications of the traditional Angoff standard-setting approach but rather as refinements or adjustments.

Two other approaches were identified for use with multiple-choice items, one based on a variation of the Nedelsky (1954) method and one based on a latent-ability conceptualization of the MCCs. The Nedelsky method has been in place for many years in one particular applied health program, whereas methods based on the latent ability concept have been in place for only a limited time, and in many cases are still in the experimental stages.

When the Nedelsky standard-setting methods are used, typically experts are instructed to eliminate options in a multiple-choice question that they believe will be obviously incorrect to the MCC. The *estimated item performance* of the MCCs is derived as a reciprocal function of the noneliminated options. This approach, therefore, assumes that the MCC will select randomly from the remaining options (or that the remaining options are equally attractive to the MCC). In an attempt to adjust for the likelihood that some options would be more appealing to the MCC, Gross (1985) introduced a variation that asks experts to provide differential weights to the remaining alternatives. This method, sometimes referred to as the Nedelsky-Gross method, is used in one operational program in the allied health field for *setting performance standards*.

Methods based on the concept of latent ability have been used or are being developed in several disciplines, including allied health, computer technology, insurance, and business. Under this paradigm, expert panelists are presented items that are indicators of varying latent or underlying abilities. The panelists' task is to identify where on the continuum, based on the evidence provided by the illustrative items, the ability level of the MCC is captured. This is sometimes done in an iterative approach. First, "marker items" from the full ability scale are presented to have the panelists identify a range where, in their opinion, the MCC's ability falls. Next, panelists are presented with additional items from that narrowed ability range. Often companion information is provided to inform the decision-making process (e.g., the impact on the proportion of candidates who would pass or fail based on the location of the performance standard).

In summary, the most prevalent method identified by the agency personnel interviewed was the Angoff standard-setting method; however, notable variations were in place. One agency uses modification of the Nedelsky approach whereby differential weights can be applied to the remaining multiple-choice options following option elimination. Some gather information about panelists' overall expectations for the percentage of items to be required for passing or the proportion of candidates who would pass. This information is not used to adjust to the resulting performance standard, but rather is shared with the panelists when the candidate performance data and the impact of the initial performance standard are reported or is used for evaluating the homogeneity of panelists' preliminary perceptions of the candidate group. Methods tied to item response theory (IRT) methods are also in place, mostly with very large programs that feel the assumptions of the model are adequately met by the program.

Open-Ended Questions

Many of the licensure and certification programs' assessments contain open-ended questions, either in the form of written essays, oral response, or observations of performance by scorers. An important consideration when working with open-ended assessments is the total number of open-ended questions that comprise the assessment package and the complexity of these questions. In some programs, the number of open-ended questions is fairly small (between 5 & 10); for others, the number is much higher (15–20 or more).

The magnitude and complexity of the total assessment have implications for the utility of some of the standard-setting approaches used with open-ended assessments. If the total number of questions and the complexity of these responses are somewhat limited, procedures that seek a holistic decision about the overall performance of the candidates can be used. When the number of questions is high, the ability of the panelists to make a holistic judgment about the overall performance becomes more difficult. In such cases, strategies that use the information on the individual questions to set an overall performance standard are needed. One such approach is to set individual performance standards on the separate questions and then aggregate these performance standards per question to obtain the cutscore on the full test.

Question by Question Methods

Several programs that use a question by question (sometimes referred to as an exercise by exercise) approach were found. A prevalent strategy employed with open-ended questions uses an analytic analysis of the probable performance of a typical MCC. In many of these applications, the scoring guidelines identify positive points assignable for specific responses. In addition, negative points can be accrued for anticipated mistakes. Through an analysis of the anticipated performance of the MCC, accruing positive and negative points, the expected score is obtained (frequently referred to as the minimum passing level [MPL] for the question). An aggregate of the MPLs across the items in the test serves as the minimum passing score for the test.

Programs that report using such a question by question approach indicated that the resulting aggregate standard often was viewed as unrealistically high. Therefore, in their view, some strategies need to be introduced to provide a more holistic view of the collective performance, not simply to represent the overall cutscore as the aggregate across the individual components. An attempt to adjust for this problem was used in a business application. Periodically, as the panelists proceeded through the test, making their question by question minimum passing score determinations, they were given information on the aggregate impact that the standard would have if the assessment consisted of just those assessments considered up to that point. The purpose of this exercise was to provide panelists with information on how the candidates actually performed, not only at the question level but also on the building aggregate. The intent was to counteract the "cascading" effect on the proportion of passing candidates as the question by question minimum passing scores were aggregated.

Another approach starts with the same basic strategy of having panelists provide an expected score for the MCC on each of the questions. The panelists are asked to envision a "typical" candidate whose skills are indicative of the MCC group. Then, either independently or as a group, the panelists determine the anticipated score of the MCCs on each question (MPL). The aggregate of these MPLs represents the panelists' initial performance standard. The panelists proceed systematically through the set of questions on the test, each time generating a question by question MPL. The next step is to have the panelists reconsider each of the questions in the test, in light of their expected performance of the MCC, and estimate what proportion of the MCC candidate pool would be able to obtain a score at or above the question cutscore. The final cutscore is obtained by summing the products of the question-level MPL and the estimated proportion passing across the questions in the test. Candidate data can be used at various points in this model (a) at the conclusion of the question by question aggregation to show the impact of the initial overall performance standard on the candidates pass–fail status, (b) after each question when the panelists are estimating the proportion of MCCs who will obtain scores at or above the question's cutscore, or (c) both.

Hambleton and Plake (1995) used an extended Angoff approach to have panelists estimate, for five exercises scored on a 4-point scale ranging from 1 (*substantially deficient or inadequate performance*) to 4 (*outstanding or exemplary performance*), the anticipated score of the MCC on each of a number of exercises. Next, panelists were asked to weight each exercise, where the weights represent the relative importance of that exercise to the overall purpose of the assessment. The product of the exercise's weight and the anticipated score for the MCC on that exercise was aggregated across the exercises to form an overall weighted minimum passing score. This approach attempts not only to determine the final cutscore for the MCC's anticipated performance on the individual exercises, but also to take into account the total makeup of the examination in a more holistic sense. Through their weights, panelists can identify more important test components to receive relatively higher emphasis in the final pass–fail decision.

Some of the programs employ a *paper selection* type of approach, whereby panelists are asked to select from a set of candidate performances the work that best typifies the performance of the MCC. In some, but not all, applications, the scores are revealed to the panelists. The task presented to the panelists is to select two papers from the set of benchmark papers that either represent or bracket the anticipated performance of the MCC. Panelists' aggregate results are presented to the panel, often followed by discussion, and then the panelists make a revised estimate of the performance of the MCC on this question. Their average value is used as the minimum passing score for the question. Critical to the success of this approach is the quality of the benchmark papers and how well they represent their intended score point. Another issue in the application of this approach is the distribution of the benchmark papers: They should be either representative of the full score range or typical of the MCC performance distribution.

In summary, the question by question methods use MPLs determined at the exercise level as the basis for setting the overall performance standard. These question-level MPLs are determined either through an analytic analysis of the points assignable to the exercise and estimation of the point total of the MCC on the question or by selecting from candidate papers the ones that are most indicative of the work of the MCC. These MPLs are aggregated to derive the final performance standard, or some adjustment is made either by weighting differentially the exercises in light of their relative importance or by providing periodic information on the impact of the aggregation in an attempt to counteract the effect of obtaining an overall passing score that is overly stringent.

Holistic Approaches

Some methods used in the licensure and certification field attempt to capture the totality of the candidates' performance by considering their overall examination performance. As previously mentioned, the utility of these approaches is limited to programs whose assessments allow for a meaningful conceptualization of the totality of a candidate's performance. Often this involves assessments with a limited number of open-ended questions.

Several programs use a contrasting groups-type approach. However, instead of using an external measure to determine the criterion groups, these programs often employ the total assessment performance as the basis for forming the contrasting groups. In this method, a panel of experts is given a subset of performances to view (this may entail, e.g., reading a number of essays, observing a series of candidate performances, or reviewing a portfolio of artifacts documenting the assessment performance). Based on the panelists' judgment of the performance status of these performances (i.e., classification of the performance as pass or fail), a determination is made of where the cutpoint should be set to best differentiate between these two performance categories. Variations on this method entail (a) having the panel work independently or collectively in making the assignment of the performances into the pass–fail categories, (b) selecting differing distributions for papers for the panel to review, and (c) employing different analytical methods to determine the location of the cutscore. Some of the programs purposely select performances to represent the full range of candidate performance, whereas others select performances in the vicinity of where they believe that the cutscore will fall (this is often determined by anticipating how the MCC will perform on the test and selecting illustrative performances from that score vicinity). Most often a straightforward regression algorithm is applied to the data to determine the cutpoint.

Another approach that addresses the holistic nature of the candidate's performance is the *judgmental policy-capturing* (JPC) standard-setting method (Jaeger, 1995). Panelists classify the overall quality of candidate performance based on profiles of scored performances across all performance exercises. This application, used most recently in operational standard-setting decisions for the National Board for Professional Teaching Standards certifications, involves a 1- to 4-point scale for overall candidate performance where, in general, 1 represents unacceptable performance that clearly does not warrant Board certification, 2 indicates a candidate performance that is inadequate for Board certification, 3 represents performance that satisfies the criteria for Board certification, and 4 signals exemplary performance that exceeds the performance criteria for Board certification. It is expected that the final standard will fall in the region of the overall scale that represents performance that is consistent with criteria for National Board Certification.

After training on the nature of the exercises and the meaning of the exercise scores, candidates are trained in the use of the policy-capturing methodology. Through a series of iterations, panelists are asked to make and, perhaps, modify their classification decisions on several candidate performance profiles. Based on a regression algorithm that attempts to capture a compensatory decision model that is consistent with each panelist's policy, weights are derived to be used in calculating a weighted average overall performance score for each candidate. The median of panelists' captured policies is used in developing a performance standard. Candidates with overall performance scores above the standard would receive certification, and those with scores below the standard would not. The final decision of the location of the performance standard involves another step where panelists focus on the profiles and overall performance scores that are in the vicinity of the scale-implied cutscore (e.g., close to 2.75). The final choice of the cutscore is then determined by the panelists' judgment of the minimally acceptable overall performance score for Board certification.

Also under the auspices of the National Board for Professional Teaching Standards, another approach that considers the profile of candidate performance was developed (Plake, Hambleton, & Jaeger, 1997). Called the *dominant profile method* (*DPM*), this approach involves having candidates, who are fully cognizant of the exercises and the meaning of the exercise scores, derive decision rules that capture their view of the score levels across the profile components necessary to warrant National Board certification. Under this approach, panelists can articulate decision rules that are complex and reflect mixed decision models. For example, they could set a conjunctive rule for part of the profile (a minimum score on a particular exercise) and compensatory rules for other parts. Once the decision rule for the "just barely acceptable" profile is established, any profile that has exercise scores that meet or exceed that profile are deemed to pass. Therefore, these *dominating profiles* are those that represent passing scores whereas other profiles of scores would be considered failures.

Three approaches for considering the candidates' overall performance in a holistic manner were identified—a contrasting groups approach and two approaches that are based on candidate score profiles. The contrasting groups approach classifies candidate performance into broad performance categories (e.g., pass–fail) and then uses empirical methods to establish the algorithm based on candidate scores that best distinguishes the groups. These groups are typically formed on the basis of overall test performance, so the criterion for group assignment is not independent of the performance on the individual questions that comprise the assessment. This is viewed as a confound, and a weakness, of this contrasting groups application.

The two profile based methods, the JPC approach and the DPM, both attempt to model decision rules of panelists for making pass–fail decisions. The JPC method does this indirectly by fitting regression-type models to the panelists' classification decisions. The DPM works toward group consensus by engaging the panelists in a series of activities to enable them to pose and modify their rule for making classification decisions. Another feature that distinguishes these profile-based methods is that the JPC method is purposefully compensatory whereas the DPM allows for conjunctive component in the panelists' performance-standard policy.

In summary, a variety of approaches have been implemented in the licensure and certification field with open-ended questions. The most frequently mentioned method involved focusing on the exercises one at a time and setting a minimum passing score on that exercise. The individual exercise-by-exercise minimum passing scores are then typically combined and used as the overall examination performance standards. Variations on this approach have been developed to provide for differential weightings of the exercises in formulating the overall passing score and for counteracting the stringency that is frequently observed when minimum passing scores are aggregated to determine the overall performance standard for the examination. The minimum passing scores are typically determined by having the panelists go through an analytical process of identifying the points on the question that would be expected to be earned by an MCC or by selecting from benchmark papers the work that exemplifies that of an MCC.

A few methods have attempted to use a more holistic (full examination) approach by focusing the standard-setting process on candidate profiles. These methods, used typically with assessments that have a few exercises, allow for the totality of candidate performance across the specific exercises to be the basis for the performance standard.

DISCUSSION OF STANDARD-SETTING METHODS FOR LICENSURE AND CERTIFICATION

For multiple-choice questions, current practice involves applications of the Angoff standard-setting method. The criticism voiced by some psychometricians (National Academy of Education, 1993; Shepard, 1995) about the validity of the item performance estimates provided by the panelists has not swayed these practitioners from the use of the Angoff methodology. The variations that are in place, in some ways, can be viewed as attempts to respond to these concerns. For example, some agencies use multiple rounds of training in an attempt to improve the panelists' abilities to (a) determine the knowledge, skills, and abilities of an MCC and (b) make accurate performance predictions. Other agencies use analytic methods to discount item performance estimates that are inconsistent with observed data. Other agencies address this issue more directly by providing item-level data by varying candidate groups, for example, the proportion of candidates in total score deciles who are able to answer the items correctly.

Some programs use IRT, which typically entail having panelists view marker items that are indicative of performance along the ability continuum; panelists select items that they feel are reflective of the minimum levels of ability required for licensure or certification. These methods, although theoretically appealing, are based on some strong assumptions. First, the ability being measured should represent a single dimension. This is often not the case with broadly construed licensure and certification fields. In other situations, where the content area is more narrow (as in some board certification areas or in some specializations in business), unidimensionality may be more readily achieved. However, often these fields have a small candidate base and are therefore limited in the sample sizes needed to obtain accurate item calibrations.

One development (not in credentialing, however) is use of the *bookmark approach* (Lewis, 1996), where test questions are presented, one per page, according to increasing levels of empirical difficulty. The panelists are instructed to place their bookmark in the location where the MCC is expected to be able to answer all the foregoing questions correctly. Several iterations are followed in determining the final location of the performance standard on the difficulty continuum. One attractive feature of this method is that the panelists view all items in the test, not just the illustrative items at certain locations on the ability continuum. Further, the method is based on empirically derived estimations of item difficulty, that can be estimated fairly well with as few as 50 to 75 observations. Item-response parameters, even with just a one-parameter model, require more than four times this sample size to obtain minimally stable estimates of difficulty.

Open-ended questions are receiving a lot of attention in the licensure and certification fields. The most common approach identified by the agencies interviewed was based on a question by question method. Variations were designed to allow for perceptions that the whole performance should be more than just the sum of the parts. Question by question MPLs are obtained either through an analytic approach or by selecting from illustrative performances those that reflect the expected performance of the MCC. This latter approach is similar conceptually to that previously discussed when marker questions are shown to illustrate the level of performance along the ability continuum. Instead of showing a question that is aligned with a level of ability, in this application, candidate work represents points on the ability continuum. The task is also conceptually similar in that the panelists are instructed to select either the level of question that represents the work of the MCC or the actual work samples that are indicative of MCC performance.

Holistic methods are designed to allow the totality of the candidates' performance, across the exercises that comprise the assessment, to be the basis for the overall pass–fail decision. Extant methods use the overall performance categorization as the basis for determining contrasting groups. Variations in the analytic method employed to determine the cutpoint that best differentiates the pass and fail groups are being developed. One of these approaches combines panelists' preconceptions in a Bayesian model to determine the cutpoint. To date, these methods have been used mostly with assessments involving only a few questions; the degree to which they can be generalized to assessments with a larger number of questions is yet to be seen. Methods under development focus on the ability to capture noncompensatory decision policies.

It is clear that there is much interest in new standard-setting methods for use with open-ended assessments. Not addressed are issues faced when the assessment program consists of both open-ended and multiple-choice components. Although one obvious approach to combining these components is to set separate cutpoints on each, this conjunctive approach is not sensitive to the relative importance of the components or to the performance distributions of the candidate group. As licensure and certification agencies expand their extant programs to involve both multiple-choice and open-ended components, it is expected that the field will need to consider ways to combine the performances across these components into a meaningful, single combinatorial performance standard.

IMPLICATION OF STANDARD-SETTING METHODS FROM THE LICENSURE AND CERTIFICATION FIELD FOR NAEP

Experience in the field of licensure and certification can provide some guidance on setting performance standards for NAEP. However, due to many of the differences between NAEP and the field of licensure and certification, generalizations should be made with extreme caution.

One very critical difference between assessments in the fields of licensure and certification and NAEP assessments is the consequence for the examinee. In licensure and certification, the candidate is directly affected: Whether the candidate passes or fails will influence, at least in part, the decision regarding his or her ability to perform or receive the benefits of the license or certificate. Therefore, the stakes for the examinee are high and candidate motivation is generally unquestioned. For students who are selected to participate in the NAEP assessments, the consequences are remote. Because individual results are not the focus of the NAEP program, the stakes for the examinee are not high, neither is there unquestioned motivation.

Some of the methods described in this article may be less effective with candidate performances that lack consistent motivation. For example, a contrasting groups approach, the basis for which is the classification of overall candidate performance as pass or fail, may be very difficult when a candidate does not give a consistent pattern of performances. It may be the case for a nonmotivated candidate that some exercises, either ones that are more appealing or are easier to answer, will show a different level of ability than those that are less interesting or more challenging. For the highly motivated candidate, the profile of performances across the tasks is expected to represent the candidate's best work, not an idiosyncratic response to specific tasks that comprise the assessment.

Another important distinction between NAEP and many licensure and certification programs is the matrix sampling of tasks included in the assessment. Although some licensure and certification programs involve some degree of sampling of tasks, the majority of the agencies interviewed used a common set of tasks for all candidates. Applications of the contrasting groups approach may be difficult under the matrix-sampling method because the basis for the assignment into a pass or fail group would need to take into account both the candidate's overall performance and the relative difficulty of the tasks comprising that candidate's overall assessment. Methods identified in the field of licensure and certification may show some promise here, especially those that involve a linking of panelists' judgments to equate performance standards across assessments or those that adjust for task difficulty based on a latent-trait model.

None of the licensure and certification programs' standard-setting procedures described in this article involve the use of multiple-level cutpoints. Typically, for licensure and certification programs, the decision is a dichotomy—either the candidate passes, and is therefore licensed or certified, or the candidate fails and is not licensed or certified. The NAEP assessment reports results in multiple levels: below basic, basic, proficient, and advanced. The concept of minimally competent, as applied in the field of licensure and certification, typically has direct, behavioral implications: The minimally competent candidate has just barely met the qualifications needed to warrant licensure or certification. Differing degrees of qualifications are not central to the standard-setting process. However, for the NAEP program, separate cutpoints are needed for those candidates whose performance is just minimally acceptable at the basic level, at the proficient level, and at the advanced level. Applications of the standard-setting approaches used in the field of licensure and certification, therefore, would need to be extended or adapted to be applicable to setting multiple cutpoints along the ability continuum. It is possible, but difficult, to imagine a single panelist whose task it is to sequentially envision candidates whose level of performance is barely acceptable, not just for one point on the ability scale but for three different decision points. The concern expressed regarding the Angoff approach (that conceptualizing a hypothetical group of candidates is difficult and making item performance estimates overly challenging) would be amplified in the situation where panelists are asked to envision not one but three different hypothetical groups of candidates, and then to make accurate item performance estimates for these specific hypothetical candidate groups.

Applying a multiclassification based decision model may make more sense in this application, as the panelists could be asked to make a single judgment based on the evaluation of the candidate's performance on a specific exercise: Does this performance meet or exceed the minimum levels of performance necessary for classification as basic, proficient, or advanced? Strategies would still need to be developed to make the decision about the cutpoint on the exercise that differentiates the candidates who are classified as basic, proficient, or advanced. This could be accomplished through multiple applications of regression-based methods.

IRT calibrations could also be used to determine the location of these multiple cutpoints. Marker questions, indicative of the performance along the latent ability continuum, could be presented, and the panelists task would be to set multiple cutpoints, one representing their perception of the ability level performance of candidates barely meeting the requirements for designations as basic, proficient, and advanced.

Another distinction between standard-setting for licensure and certification programs and NAEP is the feasibility of certain types of validity studies. It is almost never feasible in a licensure or certification setting to undertake classical validity studies. Due to the very nature of the licensure process, only persons who pass the licensure test and meet the other licensing requirements are permitted to practice. Gathering criterion data on the effectiveness or success of all candidates are neither possible or defensible on legal or moral grounds. Some licensure and certification programs gather data about expected performance of candidates from predictions by training program administrators or reports from supervisors who hire the licensed–certified candidates. In most licensure and certification applications, however, only evidence of procedural validity (Kane, 1992, 1994) is available to evaluate the accuracy of decisions based on the passing score. NAEP, on the other hand, has the potential for gathering other external achievement indicators for examinees. These achievement indicators could take the form of teacher ratings of students' achievement levels, students' performance on other achievement tests, or other information about performance in society and the workplace. The fact that provision of individual data is not an objective of the NAEP program makes some of the data recording potentially cumbersome, as data from individuals who took the NAEP assessments would need to be matched to data from other files or sources. However, these sources of validity evidence are potentially available and could lend credence to an argument about the accuracy of the achievement levels determined through a standard-setting procedure for NAEP.

The unique nature of the NAEP assessment program, with (a) the intent of reporting group, not individual, results that have little or no consequences for the examinee, (b) the matrix sampling of questions to be administered, and (c) the use of multiple cutpoints, limits the applicability to that program of many of the standard-setting methods in credentialing. There are still important models from the licensure and certification field that may be applied to the NAEP program, but the unique aspects of the NAEP program should be kept in mind when the utility of these methods for setting performance standards on NAEP assessments is considered.

ACKNOWLEDGMENTS

This article was commissioned by the Committee on the Evaluation of National and State Assessments of Educational Progress for the NAEP Achievement Levels: Setting Consensus Goals for Academic Achievement workshop, Washington, DC, December 1996. The article has not been reviewed by the Committee or by the National Research Council, and the views expressed here are solely my own.

REFERENCES

Angoff, W. H. (1971). Scales, norms, and equivalent scores. In R. L. Thorndike (Ed.), *Educational measurement,* (2nd ed., pp. 508–600). Washington, DC: American Council on Education.

Beuk, C. H. (1984). A method for reaching a compromise between absolute and relative standards on examinations. *Journal of Educational Measurement, 22,* 263–269.

Browning, A. H., Bugbee, A. C., & Mullins, M. A. (Eds.). (1996). *Certification: A NOCA handbook.* Washington, DC: National Organization for Competency Assurance.

Cizek, G. J. (1996). Standard-setting guidelines. *Educational Measurement: Issues and Practice, 15*(1), 13–21, 12.

de Gruijter, D. N. M. (1985). Compromise methods for establishing examination standards. *Journal of Educational Measurement, 30,* 93–106.

Dillon, G. F. (1996). The expectations of standard-setting judges. *The CLEAR Exam Review, 7,* 22–26.

Dillon, G. F., Swanson, D. B., Nungester, R. J., Peskin, E., & Ross, L. P. (1993, April). *A system for training standard-setting judges using repeated exercises, questionnaires, and unique data formats.* Paper presented at the annual meeting of the American Educational Research Association, Atlanta, GA.

Fidler, J. R. (1996). *A survey of examination-related practices employed by credentialing agencies.* Unpublished manuscript.

Gross, L. J. (1985). Setting cutoff scores on credentialing examinations: A refinement in the Nedelsky procedure. *Evaluation & the Health Professions, 8,* 469–493.

Hambleton, R. K., & Plake, B. S. (1995). Using an extended Angoff procedure to set standards on complex performance assessments. *Applied Measurement in Education, 8,* 41–55.

Hofstee, W. K. B. (1983). A case for compromise in educational selection and grading. In S. B. Anderson & J. S. Helmick (Eds.), *On educational testing* (pp. 109–127). San Francisco: Jossey-Bass.

Mills, C. N. (1994). Setting cut scores. In J. C. Impara (Ed.), *Licensure testing: Purposes, procedures, and practices* (pp. 219–252). Lincoln, NE: Buros Institute of Mental Measurements.

Mills, C. N., & Melican, G. J. (1988). Estimating and adjusting cutoff scores: Features of selected methods. *Applied Measurement in Education, 1,* 261–275.

National Academy of Education (1993). *Setting performance standards for student achievement.* Stanford, CA: Author.

Nedelsky, L. (1954). Absolute grading standards for objective tests. *Educational and Psychological Measurement, 14,* 3–19.

Plake, B. S., Hambleton, R. K., & Jaeger, R. M. (1997). A new standard-setting method for performance assessments: The dominant profile judgment method and some field test results. *Educational and Psychological Measurement, 57,* 400–411.

Shepard, L. A. (1995, October). *Implications for standard-setting of the NAE evaluation of NAEP.* Paper presented at the joint conference on standard-setting for large scale assessments, National Assessment Governing Board, National Center for Educational Statistics, Washington, DC.

Sireci, S. A., & Biskin, B. H. (1992). Measurement practices in national licensing examination programs: A survey. *The CLEAR Exam Review, 3,* 21–25.

Lessons for the National Assessment of Educational Progress From Military Standard Setting

Lawrence M. Hanser
RAND
Santa Monica, California

The U.S. military services have a long history of setting and using standards. It is important to understand how military and education contexts differ if one is to transfer any standard-setting lessons from the miliary to the public education sector. First, the military system regularly rotates personnel from operational to training positions and back again. This provides a natural feedback loop along which information is passed to assist the training establishment in knowing its successes and failures. Second, military standards are ultimately linked as closely as possible to real-world outcomes. Military standards matter, and especially so to trainers whose lives may later rely on the abilities of their former students. The major distinction and lesson to be learned from military experience is that to be useful, standards must be grounded in real-world outcomes that affect the lives of educators. National Assessment of Educational Progress standards currently appear to be lacking on both counts.

The U.S. military services have a long history of setting and using standards. Unfortunately, having a long history does not mean that they have developed a magic bullet for setting standards that is secreted away in the bowels of the Pentagon. Nonetheless, this considerable experience in setting and using standards may offer some lessons for National Assessment of Educational Progress (NAEP) standard setting.

In addition to standards that are applied to people or groups of people, the military services apply standards to the design and manufacture of equipment, whether hardware or software. Although it may be instructive to consider how

---

Requests for reprints should be sent to Lawrence M. Hanser, RAND, 1700 Main Street, P.O. Box 2138, Santa Monica, CA 90407–2138.

equipment standards are set within the general rubric of standard setting, I confine myself in this article to briefly review the development and use of standards related to military personnel.

I will follow the life cycle of a soldier[1] to review the points at which the military services use personnel standards and discuss why and how the various standards are set and used. Finally, I will present my perspective on the relevance of standard-setting techniques used by the military services for NAEP standard setting vis-à-vis NAEP achievement levels. I will try in this brief article not to revisit familiar issues related to standard setting, except insofar as they are distinctly relevant to my discussion of standard setting in the military.

PUTTING MILITARY AND NAEP STANDARD SETTING IN CONTEXT

In thinking about how standard setting in the military may be relevant to standard setting in NAEP, it is important to recognize the different contexts within which the standards are set. In many ways, the military services are a closed system. The services provide the bulk of their own training and largely control the conditions in which on-the-job performance occurs. Furthermore, there is constant movement of personnel within the system that cross-fertilizes the components of the system. Recruiters and drill sergeants come from within the ranks of operating units and return to them. Training managers and platform instructors come from within the ranks of operating units and return to them. Soldiers, seamen, airmen, and marines in operating units have all risen up through the ranks, beginning as raw recruits in basic training of one form or another. The highest ranking generals began their military careers as lieutenants or captains, and the highest ranking noncommissioned officers have been privates, airmen, or seamen.

The education establishment, whether private or public, is a closed system but in a way that is different from the military services. First, except for private institutions, elementary and secondary schools are open to all. Second, the interests of students and parents are paramount in choosing programs of study, whereas the military places an individual into a training program in which that individual has been predicted to succeed. Third, it is highly unlikely that a teacher will have had experience in the career that his or her students eventually choose to enter. Finally, once a student leaves school, the subsequent performance of the student most likely will never affect the school. In short, schools are relatively isolated from the world of work and the consequences of the quality of the education they provide, whereas military training centers and operating units are tightly integrated.

---

[1] Although I use the U.S. Army term *soldier* throughout this article, it should be taken more generally to refer to personnel in any of the military services, including seamen, airmen, and marines.

These are stark contrasts between the military and education contexts that have two important effects on standard setting. First, there are substantial differences in the external information that educators and military trainers have available for setting standards. The flow of personnel through military assignments and careers means that field operating units and training centers have a natural feedback loop for information regarding the relations between training and performance as well as firsthand knowledge of the performance of trainees in later job assignments. Educators typically do not have the luxury of hands-on experience, let alone recent hands-on experience, in anything but education. This hampers their ability to set standards that are relevant outside the sphere of education itself. Military trainers, on the other hand, have all had direct field experience, and may cycle from field operating units to training institutions several times within the span of a career.

Second, and perhaps more important, there are differences in the incentives that individuals in military and education settings have for setting meaningful standards and ensuring that students achieve them. A soldier's life may depend on setting the right standard and ensuring that trainees surpass it. It is hard to imagine that a math teacher, high school principal, or superintendent experiences quite the same reality.

This is not to say that there are no lessons from military standard setting that are relevant for NAEP. Indeed, if we assume that the same scientific techniques for standard setting are freely available to all institutions, then what differentiates one from another in its success with setting standards, or its decision as to how to set standards? Perhaps if we can agree that at least some of the differences between the military and education sectors are a function of the differing contexts within which standards are set and must operate, we have at least identified avenues to consider for improving the setting of standards in education. I shall return to this topic later.

WHAT STANDARDS ARE SET AND APPLIED TO MILITARY PERSONNEL?

There are standards for individual soldiers, seamen, and airmen as well as for teams, squads, platoons, squadrons, brigades, wings, fleets, armies, and so forth. One may even recognize that there are standards, although in constant flux, for the entire U.S. military force. At one extreme, each individual soldier must meet standards for basic weapon marksmanship. At the other extreme, the entirety of our military forces must currently meet a "readiness" standard of being able to fight and succeed in two simultaneous multiple regional conflicts. Each of these standards has been developed and clearly laid out by the military establishment.

As in NAEP, the military establishment must both set the standards and develop methods for determining whether those standards have been met. For example, to meet the standard for marksmanship, the military services must decide which targets and what proportion of targets individual soldiers must be able to hit, and under what conditions. To meet the standard for readiness, the Department of Defense must decide how much training and transportation capacity must exist to deploy in a timely manner with enough force to succeed in two simultaneous multiple-regional conflicts.

Also, as for NAEP, the standards that are set in the military are meaningful only to the degree to which they have external validity. Do standards for math performance have any value if not connected to identified external outcomes?[2] Unfortunately, there is little evidence of external validity for NAEP standards. Targets on a rifle range are important for soldiers to hit only if hitting them means that soldiers will hit targets on a battlefield—battles are not fought on rifle ranges. Furthermore, concrete and objective external validity is difficult if not impossible to establish, whether one is setting math standards for eighth-grade students or setting standards for speed in assembling the breech block of an artillery piece. Higher scores and shorter times are almost always better, but how high a score and how fast a time marks proficiency as compared to mastery?

RECRUITMENT AND ENLISTMENT

The first stages in a military career, whether that career lasts for 4 years or 30 years, are recruitment and enlistment. As in other personnel selection settings, screening (i.e., the application of standards) is used from the outset. For the military services, this means that standards are first applied when recruiters differentially value specific characteristics in the individuals they recruit, for example, high school graduates versus nongraduates. Recruiters spend more time on individuals whom they are told have higher value to the services. Part of the emphasis for recruiters is the result of individual recruiting goals that may specify a goal of one high school graduate for each month, but all recruiters are familiar with and influenced by the services enlistment standards.

Entry-level standards for all military personnel focus on three characteristics: (a) aptitude for military occupations; (b) adaptability to military life; and (c) moral character. For enlisted positions, recruiters concentrate on whether an individual will graduate or graduated from high school as a reflection of aptitude and adaptability. Criminal records, frequent brushes with the legal system, or self-admitted illegal drug use are considered reflections of a lack of moral character that may lead to continued illegal behavior while in the service.

For officer commissioning, the most common indicator of aptitude is college degree status. Adaptability is reflected in the individual's having obtained a high school diploma and by successful completion of summer boot camp during or

---

[2] I do not wish to imply that I restrict the meaning of external outcomes to observable performance. It seems sufficient to me to have an enlightened citizenry as an explicitly defined external goal.

immediately after college. Morals are indicated in the same way as for enlisted applicants.

Because they are entry standards and not posteducation or training standards (like NAEP), one may be tempted to dismiss recruitment and enlistment standards as irrelevant to the NAEP standard-setting process. However, they are standards for the performance of individuals prior to entry, and in that sense the methods used to set them are relevant and may be instructive.

SETTING RECRUITING AND ENLISTMENT STANDARDS

As I have already noted, the military services are interested in enlisting individuals who exhibit the capacity to complete occupational training and to perform successfully in military occupations in military settings. Military recruiting and enlistment standards are based on an individual's predicted performance or success in the service.

One aspect of success in the military is defined by completing training and remaining in the service until one's original term of enlistment ends. Successful completion of training signals that an individual has the capacity to pass the requisite "can-do" standards for being in the service. But successful completion of training also signals that an individual possesses the requisite "will-do" capacity to adapt to a military lifestyle.

Another aspect of success is defined as how well one performs in training and later in a field assignment. Some individuals will barely pass training, whereas others sail easily through training. Some individuals will barely meet requirements for the pace of promotions, and others will receive early promotions.[3] Thus, there are both absolute measures (i.e., complete vs. fail; stay vs. leave) and normative measures (i.e., barely pass vs. lead the class; slower vs. faster promotion rates).

It is probably an understatement to say that hundreds of research reports have been written about recruiting and enlistment standards. Much of this literature does not appear in professional academic journals but rather can be found as technical reports published either by the Department of Defense or by contractors (e.g., Vineberg & Joyner, 1981; Welsh et al., 1990). For example, Vineberg and Joyner reviewed 143 published reports that examined the relation between test scores and performance in military occupations. Furthermore, most of this literature focuses on establishing the validity of various instruments for predicting performance in training or on the job, rather than on setting standards for either test performance or job performance.

---

[3]The military services require that individuals achieve certain pay-grade levels by certain points in time, or they are released from service. These requirements are typically not a factor in the initial term of enlistment but become increasingly important as military careers lengthen. For example, an officer who has not reached the rank of colonel by a certain number of years of service is released from service.

Standards for recruiting and enlistment have always been set on the basis of staff recommendation and judgment. The function of research, rather than on what the standards may be, has tended to focus on the outcomes associated with different levels of standards. What is the likely outcome in terms of measures of interest (e.g., attrition or job performance) if a given standard is set and used? This information is then provided to decision makers who choose the standard to apply.

One interesting result of this focus on providing useful information to decision makers was the development of the *dollar criterion* (Brogden & Taylor, 1950). Literally, what are the cost and value of using a specific test for selection and classification? Or, what are the cost and value of applying a given standard? Even today, research on standard setting in the military continues to focus on understanding the costs and benefits of given standards as a means for choosing standards. However, today's research has begun to examine increasingly objective methods for setting standards. For example, Armor et al. (1982) reasoned that the propensity of recruits to remain in the service (indexed by high school graduation status) and their ability to perform in military occupations (predicted from validity studies relating Armed Services Vocational Aptitude Battery [ASVAB] test scores to measures of job performance) could be combined in a cost-performance trade-off model that would maximize the number of qualified man-days for the lowest cost and yield an optimal enlistment standard. Obviously this research could not have been done without a basis in validity research showing the relations between high school graduation status and attrition and between ASVAB and performance.[4]

In a similar example of this kind of focus, Smith and Hogan (1994) reported on the development of a mathematical model that solves for recruiting and enlistment standards based on personnel costs and specified performance goals, where the linkage of test performance to job performance has been statistically established, and standards of job performance have also been established.

The model that Smith and Hogan (1994) reported is relevant to informing NAEP standard setting by highlighting the importance of certain kinds of information that as yet may be largely unavailable for use in NAEP—concrete external validity that test scores are related to performance of interest and values associated with certain levels of performance. These are the basis of Smith and Hogan's model. Their model literally states that if we desire y amount of performance at minimal cost, the profile of group scores on the ASVAB must be x. In this sense, military researchers are two steps ahead of their education counterparts as the result of having substantial criterion-related validity research on which to build standard-setting models. This

---

[4]There is, of course, a near infinite regression of standards if one looks carefully at this research. For example, *qualified man-days* is defined as both being in the service and achieving a passing score on a test of job knowledge. Hence, one may wish to examine how the passing score on the test of job knowledge is set. Of course, the same is true when considering a contrasting group's technique for setting standards—how is the standard set for distinguishing the contrasting groups?

is not to say that military researchers have solved the general standard-setting problem, only that they may have more data with which to work, and data that have greater connections to external realities.

Obviously Smith and Hogan (1994) used expert judgments as the basis of valuing certain levels of performance, and these judgments are imperfect, as they are in NAEP. Wise (1994) reported on five different judgment methods that were used with differing success in setting standards for the performance of army soldiers. The single rater reliabilities ranged from $r_{xx} = .42$ to $r_{xx} = .07$. The highest reliabilities were for methods based on asking judges to rate minimum acceptable scores for different proficiency levels on types of tasks, given an exemplary list of tasks. Single judge reliabilities were lower when judges were asked to rate minimum acceptable scores for different proficiency levels for each specific task—not unlike the judgment task used by NAEP.

In any case, the military establishment's research that supports recruiting and enlistment standards points to the necessity of certain kinds of underlying information that may not be available for NAEP. We also begin to see philosophical differences between NAEP standard setting and the military's view of standard setting. Military decision makers always ask what difference the standard will make and how much it will cost. They also recognize explicitly that some standards are arbitrary and set on the basis of judgment and some are more absolute and objective.

Reasonable questions can be raised at this point. First, would it make sense for military enlistment standards to be set following the NAEP-employed model of standard setting by having academic and vocational high school teachers make judgments about individual ASVAB items? How is this fundamentally different from what NAEP has done? If this would not make sense, why not, and why does it make sense for NAEP to use that method? Second, could NAEP follow the military services' techniques of examining the outcomes and costs associated with different scores, and if not, would it make sense and what would it take?

INDIVIDUAL SKILL TRAINING

Every individual who enters military service undergoes individual skill training that is not only primarily vocational in focus but also may include cognitive skills such as math and problem solving. Furthermore, no soldier is allowed to join a unit without passing individual skill training. One exception to this is that navy recruits may be assigned general duty on shipboard as seamen for a period of time prior to undergoing occupational specialty training.

Minimum standards of performance in training determine who passes and is eligible for assignment to an operational unit (e.g., navy ship, air force squadron, army battalion, marine corps battalion). However, unlike in public school systems, part of the entrance screening process is based on predicted ability to pass skill training. As a result, failure rates are low and performance standards in training are met by almost all. The attrition that occurs during military training is more often from an individual's failure to adapt to a military environment than from inability to pass the technical aspects of training.

Soldiers have incentives to perform better than the minimum level required to pass training. Many are intrinsically motivated to perform well, and high performers are often rewarded with an early promotion—money in the pocket. Failure in training results in either a reassignment to a different occupation and different training or an invalidation of the soldier's enlistment contract and release from service. During periods of involuntary enlistment (i.e., the draft), soldiers had an incentive to fail training to be relieved of service, but the all-volunteer force of the past 20 years means that recruits have an incentive to pass training to stay in the service, unless the individual recruit has difficulty adapting to service life and wishes to be released.

SETTING INDIVIDUAL SKILL TRAINING STANDARDS

The process of developing individual skill training in the military services is driven by a method called *Instructional Systems Development* (*ISD*; Interservice Training Review Organization [ITRO], 1975a). In the civilian sector, ISD has been implemented as *Developing a Curriculum,* or more commonly *DACUM* (Kosidlak, 1987). DACUM analogs of ISD are widely used by community colleges and vocational and technical schools for developing systems of vocational training, including standards for passing.

ISD has five phases (analyze, design, develop, implement, and control) that begin with job analysis and include development of objectives and instructional materials, implementation of instruction, and feedback loops for evaluating and revising training. The part of ISD that speaks to standard setting is the development of *terminal learning objectives* (*TLOs*) during the design phase (ITRO, 1975b, p. 6).

One component of a TLO is the standard of performance that must be achieved on the task for a soldier to pass. To the fullest extent possible, the standards of performance on a TLO are designed to mirror field job performance standards for the task, including testing conditions. Because each task to be trained is clearly linked to performance on the job in the field, setting the standard of performance to be achieved at the end of training is relatively straightforward—that is, what is the standard of performance in the field?[5] ITRO (1975b, p. 15) lists six types of standards that may be set for TLOs. They include (a) referring to a standard operating procedure, (b) implying the standard of no error, (c) specifying minimum acceptable

---

[5]Standards of performance on the job in the field may themselves be the product of judgments on the part of strategical, tactical, and occupational experts. For example, the standard of performance for a tank crew may be some number of seconds to fire once a target is identified. Clearly there is room for disagreement among experts as to what that figure should be. Nonetheless, once that figure is specified for field performance, trainers can use that same standard to assess whether a trainee is able to meet it.

level of performance, (d) specifying the time requirements, (e) specifying the rate of production, and (f) specifying qualitative requirements. ITRO further specifies that good standards should specify the level of completeness of task performance, the level of accuracy of task performance, and the time allowed for task performance.

All individual training in the military services is tied directly to the skills and abilities that are needed to perform in the field, whether it is training to operate a nuclear reactor on a submarine, training to pilot a stealth bomber, or training to be an infantry soldier. Training is task oriented; ISD is the model that the services generally follow in the design and development of training, and it is the model that the services generally follow in setting standards for passing training. The expected level of performance at the end of formal training is that of an apprentice who has been introduced to most tasks required to be performed by entry-level workers in the occupation, and who has mastered only the most basic tasks. Further on-the-job training will focus on mastering additional tasks needed for achieving greater levels of occupational skill.

Unlike NAEP, the military services have the benefit of relatively clear external outcomes within their closed system as the basis for setting training standards. Also, individuals who set the standards for performance in training have clear shared visions of occupational proficiency that derive from shared experiences.

If we compare NAEP and military standard setting in the context of individual skill training, we can again see how contextual differences may be important. Military skill training is intended to narrow the variability among individual performers by ensuring that all trainees master the minimum required skills for an entry-level assignment. Some tasks are performed until a student achieves mastery, and some are included only for the purpose of familiarity, not skill in performance. In this context, differentiating basic proficiency from advanced proficiency has less meaning and certainly less importance than developing mastery in the set of minimum required skills—the concept of minimum required skill has meaning and value for the military because it is based on identified field performance requirements. It seems to me that applying the Angoff method would make little sense in this context because a proficient soldier would be expected to pass every trained task and a task would be included in training only if entry-level soldiers were required to exhibit proficiency in it. For most military tasks the concept of domain sampling has little meaning, so a proficient soldier passes a test of the task and soldiers who are not proficient fail.[6]

---

[6]Consider rifle marksmanship as a unique example. Every soldier must qualify with an individual weapon whether it is a rifle or sidearm. Obviously, qualifying does not require that a soldier hit every target, but rather some proportion of different kinds of targets. Setting the minimum qualifying score and scores that identify levels of proficiency above that is an exercise in judgment probably dating back at least to World War II. As a colleague put it recently, this was probably a "line drawn in the sand," without benefit of a formalized model of standard setting.

UNIT TRAINING AND PERFORMANCE

For many individuals, military careers consist primarily of individual performance (e.g., clerks, mechanics, cooks). That is, if they perform their individual tasks successfully, the task is performed successfully. On the other hand, the performance of many soldiers is meaningful only in a group context (e.g., infantrymen, aircrews). That is, many tasks are group tasks. In this case, the successful performance of one individual may be overshadowed by the poor performance of others, or vice versa.

Unit-level training for ground combat units tends to be considerably less standardized than individual training. For the most part, it occurs in field settings and is left to unit commanders and their staffs to develop. This is not to say that all unit-level training is ad hoc. All of the services have more formal and relatively standardized unit-level drills or training exercises of one sort or another that are practiced by the unit as a whole. These may be exercises to prepare air force units for deployment, or calls to general quarters for the crew of a navy vessel, or a passage of lines for an infantry and tank task force. Like individual training, these exercises can be very concrete and task oriented. For example, an air force fighter squadron may be required to generate a certain number of sorties of a given configuration within a fixed period of time to be considered to have met a standard for being mission qualified.

SETTING UNIT TRAINING AND PERFORMANCE STANDARDS

Standards for unit training are applied primarily to group performance or to individual performance that is on the critical path for group performance. For example, a single rifleman missing his target does not necessarily lead to failure of a squad in its mission. On the other hand, if the squad leader does not get his squad to the correct location, the squad fails in its task and the platoon or company may also fail. In the first case, the individual standard of performance is not so important, unless the majority also fail. In the second case, the failure of a single individual to meet a standard of performance has consequences for the entire group.

Unit training and performance standards are usually set by elements of the individual services' training commands, such as the U.S. Army Armor Center and School that is an element of the U.S. Army's Training and Doctrine Command. These centers are staffed by military personnel with expertise in the relevant occupations and by supporting civilian personnel. Some standards, such as bombing accuracy for pilots, may have straightforward criteria associated with the effect of the weapon itself. For example, the standard for at least 30 years after World War II for dropping a "dumb" bomb was to hit within a 145-foot circle around the target.

Most standards, however, have been set on the basis of expert judgment followed by constant refinement as weapons and tactics have changed. A rifle squad today may reach its designated position faster and more accurately using global positioning satellite equipment than in the past when maps and compasses were de rigueur, and standards for training and performance change to reflect that technology.

The reader may begin to see a pattern in how the military considers and sets standards—judgment and refinement of the standard tied to field outcomes. If field commanders note a discrepancy between the standards of performance that are applied in training and the standards of performance that are critical in the field, feedback mechanisms are built in to the system to bring about change. First, as I have noted, soldiers rotate from field to training assignments on a regular basis and take their field experiences with them to their assignments as trainers and training developers. Second, the services sponsor conferences focused around weapon systems or types of units (e.g., armor), so that field personnel and trainers can identify discrepancies between current standards and what is required by current practice. Third, changes to standards are routinely staffed to field units for comment prior to publication.

COMPARING NAEP AND MILITARY STANDARD-SETTING MODELS

The question at hand is not whether the NAEP method of standard setting would be appropriate for military use, but rather what may NAEP learn from the way the military sets standards. Still, I believe that considering what it would mean to use NAEP methods to set military standards is instructive in understanding the differences between how NAEP sets standards and how the military sets standards.

There are many details that one can argue about with regard to the various standards that the military services set and apply, and there are many arguments within the military establishment over standards because military personnel recognize the arbitrary nature of most standards. As a result, unless outcomes can be clearly and objectively quantified, expert judgment is relied on almost exclusively, to the point that it is very difficult to intrude on a single field commander's final judgment as to what constitutes acceptable performance.

To my knowledge, no standards are set in the military by using a detailed test-centered approach such as the Angoff method. Why is this? I think it is because tasks, seemingly reasonable military analogs for NAEP test items, are more immediately concrete and externally valid than NAEP test items. Consider bomb dropping as an example. It does not make sense to set the size of a bomb circle on which to judge bombing proficiency based on a priori judgments about how large a circle a proficient pilot should be able to hit—if a bomb falls outside a certain radius, defined by the bomb's characteristics, it is ineffective and by definition the pilot is not sufficiently proficient at that task.[7]

Another analog for NAEP test items is ASVAB items. Would it make sense to set enlistment standards on ASVAB by using Angoff or similar methods? A complete analog to what NAEP planned for itself would be to have high school academic and vocational teachers together with experienced military personnel follow the Angoff method of examining and making judgments about individual ASVAB items and to use those judgments to set enlistment standards on ASVAB. Frankly, that scenario seems unthinkable to me. This is because Angoff and similar methods turn the standard-setting process, as practiced by the military, on its head. In NAEP, the connection between test performance and an unspecified externally relevant criterion exists only in the heads of the NAEP standards setters, who are generally lacking in that externally relevant experience. As a result, NAEP standards have no clear external meaning. Although the chain of evidence for military standards may often be weakly specified, standards are always connected to externally relevant military performance.

As another example, consider the development of standards for performance in military training. If we applied the NAEP method to setting standards for performance in military training, complete fidelity to the method that NAEP used would require that military trainers who set the training standards could be quite divorced from field experience. They could be experts in training pilots, tank crewmen, and shipboard boiler operators, but may not actually be pilots, tank crewmen or boiler operators, and may be bereft of experience as to what constituted proficiency in the field. Such a scenario would also be unacceptable for military standard setting.

LESSONS FOR NAEP STANDARD SETTING

What is there of practical value in military standard setting that can be applied to NAEP? I have come to believe that the differences are as much philosophical as technical and may be largely the result of differing contexts. I was struck by the following quotation from Bourque and Hambleton (1993):

> In fact, the composition of the panel proved to be a problem. The stakeholder group nominees, although expert in their own area, came with national agendas, and they raised issues and questions that needed responses. *This took away from valuable training time, and distracted panel members from the main task at hand: rating NAEP items* [italics added]. ... It was hypothesized that teacher educators would produce standards with less variability because teachers are more likely to share a common

---

[7]This is not to say that such standards are so straightforward as to be unquestioned. However, these questions are raised and answered in the development and field testing of systems, so that by the time a system is fielded, there is little question of where the cause of inadequate field performance lies.

understanding of students' performance as well as their achievement levels. In fact, the teacher educators in the replication study did produce what seemed to be more defensible standards. (p. 43)

This statement is to me a huge red flag that something is wrong, for it seems that although stakeholders were saying that standards developed by the chosen process would be inappropriate, the standard-setting juggernaut pressed on and stakeholders were largely excluded. In their conclusions, Bourque and Hambleton (1993, pp. 46–47) stated that constituencies need to be involved in the process and to "buy-in" to the process. I would suggest that the experience of the military is even stronger in that constituent communities must own the process if they are to be part of the process.

In my judgment, there are two things that would allow this to happen. First, the lines between teachers and constituent communities need to be blurred. The military services do this as a matter of routine personnel rotation policy. As for NAEP, as long as teachers and stakeholders perceive themselves as representing distinct interests with different agendas, it will be difficult for either group to accept the decisions, or perhaps even the leadership, of the other. As highlighted in the quotation from Bourque and Hambleton (1993), stakeholders were deemed by those in control of the standard-setting process to be unable to set standards and to detract from the process that had been chosen to set the standards. The result fundamentally was to exclude noneducators, even though other statements indicated that there were later found to be no substantial differences in the standards set with or without their input.[8] To the extent that the teaching profession provides opportunities for teachers to work in other capacities in other organizations, and that other organizations provide opportunities for their personnel to teach in schools, it will be easier for teachers and stakeholders to join together in the standard-setting process. Because this may be unrealistic, increased opportunities could be created for teachers and stakeholders to work together before, during, and after the standard-setting process so that there are no differences in agendas and unity of mind as to how the standards will be set.

Second, standards that are relatively context free are difficult to set and difficult to accept. To the extent that standards in the military are not linked to some observable external outcome of value to the user community (i.e., field operating

---

[8] I found it interesting to read in Bourque and Garrison (1991) that

[A] thorough analysis of the two sets of data (one from Vermont/Washington and one from the replication/validation study) demonstrated that the results and recommendations from the two initiatives were not substantially different. Therefore, after reviewing the data and considering the recommendations, the Board adopted the achievement levels from the replication/validation study for use in reporting the 1990 NAEP mathematics results. *These standards represent the judgment of NAGB after careful consideration of the recommendations of classroom teachers, education experts, and interested members of the general public* [italics added]. (p. 11)

units), they are dead on arrival. Disagreement among teachers as to the standards, as evidenced by standard deviations of judges' final standards, is sufficient by itself to indicate that the standards (basic, proficient, and advanced) were poorly linked to external outcomes. This point highlights the importance of including stakeholder communities in the entire standard-setting process. By this I do not mean that stakeholders be persuaded of the appropriateness of the method chosen to set standards, but rather that they become part of the process of choosing or developing the method used to set the standards.

Having said this, however, I wonder that perhaps NAEP has not benefitted from a clear vision of what the standards are to represent. There may be at least two observable outcomes that have become confused in NAEP standards. The first is some pure concept of subject matter proficiency in a defined domain of knowledge. Standards reflecting subject matter proficiency ought to be the primary province of educators. Unfortunately, the questions that many have already posed about the quality of NAEP achievement standards seem to indicate that subject matter proficiency has not been well defined, understood, or both by those educators who are setting NAEP achievement standards.

The second observable outcome is the meaning of proficiency that connects to the world outside the classroom. For this, one must turn to parents, businessmen, and postsecondary education and training institutions. It is not clear that these connections are well enough understood to benefit NAEP. In the military, the lines between training and later performance are direct because they are designed to be so. In the civilian sector, the lines between education and later performance are tenuous and not easily understood. Proficiency in this context of observable outcomes needs to be specified—proficiency for what?

The military establishment has the luxury of attending to only the latter. As I have said previously in different words, military standards exist because they are tied to observable outcomes, and the military establishment has a good shared understanding of what those outcomes are. Military researchers have taken this to heart as well in constructing population-based models for standards, examples of which I have previously noted (Armor et al., 1982; Smith & Hogan, 1994). These models offer some thoughts for the future of NAEP, but they may be premature until such time as the links between education and the world outside of education are better understood and better delineated.

ACKNOWLEDGMENTS

This article was commissioned by the Committee on the Evaluation of National and State Assessments of Educational Progress for the NAEP Achievement Levels: Setting Consensus Goals for Academic Achievement workshop, Washington, DC, December 1996. The views expressed here are solely my own.

REFERENCES

Armor, D. J., Fernandez, R. L., Bers, K., Schwarzbach, D. S., Moore, S. C., & Cutler, L. (1982). *Recruit aptitudes and army job performance: Setting enlistment standards for infantrymen.* Santa Monica, CA: RAND.
Bourque, M. L., & Garrison, H. H. (1991). *The LEVELS of mathematics achievement: Initial performance for the 1990 NAEP mathematics assessment. Vol. 1. National and state summaries.* Washington, DC: National Assessment Governing Board.
Bourque, M. L., & Hambleton, R. K. (1993). Setting performance standards on the national assessment of educational progress. *Measurement and Evaluation in Counseling and Development, 26,* 41–47.
Brogden, H. E., & Taylor, E. K. (1950). The dollar criterion: Applying the cost accounting concept to criterion construction. *Personnel Psychology, 3,* 133–154.
Interservice Training Review Organization. (1975a). *Interservice procedures for instructional systems development: Executive summary and model.* Pensacola, FL: Naval Education and Training Center.
Interservice Training Review Organization. (1975b). *Interservice procedures for instructional systems development: Phase II, design.* Pensacola, FL: Naval Education and Training Center.
Kosidlak, J. G. (1987). DACUM: An alternative job analysis tool. *Personnel, 64,* 14–21.
Smith, D. A., & Hogan, P. F. (1994). The accession quality/cost performance trade-off model. In B. F. Green & A. S. Mavor (Eds.), *Modeling cost and performance for military enlistment* (pp. 105–128). Washington, DC: National Academy Press.
Vineberg, R., & Joyner, J. N. (1981). *Prediction of job performance: Review of military studies.* Alexandria, VA: Human Resources Research Organization.
Welsh, J. R., Trent, L. M., Nakasone, R. I., Fairbank, B. A., Kucikas, S. K., & Sawin, L. L. (1990). *Annotated bibliography of armed services vocational aptitude battery (ASVAB) validity studies.* Brooks Air Force Base, TX: Air Force Human Resources Laboratory.
Wise, L. L. (1994). Setting performance goals for the DOD linkage model. In B. F. Green & A. S. Mavor (Eds.), *Modeling cost and performance for military enlistment* (pp. 37–60). Washington, DC: National Academy Press.

The Recommended Dietary Allowances: Can They Inform the Development of Standards of Academic Achievement?

Jeanne P. Goldberg
School of Nutrition Science and Policy
Tufts University

The Recommended Dietary Allowances are the most widely used standard in the field of nutrition. They have served for over 50 years as the basis for fundamental food and nutrition policies that affect every American. A review of the evolution of these standards provides guidance for the development of standards of academic achievement that will be accepted by a broad range of users. The development of standards is an iterative process, and regular review and revision must be anticipated and planned for. Controversies are most likely to arise in the absence of unequivocal data and the need to substitute judgment, no matter how well informed. Finally, if standards are to be widely accepted, some level of consensus is critical. Therefore, the process of establishing them must be open to those who are interested.

For more than 50 years, the Recommended Dietary Allowances (RDAs) have served as the basis for fundamental food and nutrition policy decisions that affect every American. The RDAs are integral to food and nutrition policy in this country. They serve as the yardstick to measure the effects of any new food program and any shift in nutrition policy on the dietary intakes of the population (Food and Nutrition Board [FNB], 1994). The RDAs have changed and will continue to change as newer information becomes available.

In this article, I provide a brief review of more than five decades of experience in interpretation of the science and the scholarly debate associated with the publication of successive revisions of the RDAs. Although the challenges of standard setting are quite different for nutrition and education, a review of the

---

Request for reprints should be sent to Jeanne P. Goldberg, School of Nutrition Science and Policy, Tufts University, 126 Curtis Street, Medford, MA 02155.

evolution of the RDAs provides some important lessons about process that may be instructive in deliberations about the development and implementation of performance measures in education.

EVOLUTION OF THE CONCEPT

The first RDAs were produced in 1941 by the Committee on Food and Nutrition, established by the National Research Council to advise government agencies on all problems relating to food and nutrition in the U.S. population and especially on feeding the armed forces. They were published in 1943.

The report of the first committee explains that the RDAs were designed "with the objective of 'providing standards to serve as a goal for good nutrition' and as a yardstick against which to measure progress toward that goal" (FNB, 1943, p. 1). The 6-page document defined the RDAs for the various dietary essentials for people of different ages. The term *recommended allowances* instead of "standards" was used to avoid any implication of finality (FNB, 1943). Since the first edition, each publication has noted the insufficiency of data with which to make judgments.

Text for the third edition (FNB, 1948), published just 5 years later, carefully reflected committee deliberations and the rationale for key decisions. It specified that "[t]he recommendations are not called requirements because they are intended to represent not merely the literal (minimal) requirements of average individuals, but levels high enough to cover substantially all individual variations in the requirements of normal people" (p. 4). The clear definition that has remained essentially unchanged for 20 years first appeared in the eighth edition (National Research Council [NRC], 1974):

> The Recommended Dietary Allowances are the levels of intake of essential nutrients considered, in the judgment of the Food and Nutrition Board on the basis of available scientific knowledge, to be adequate to meet the known nutritional needs of practically all healthy persons. (p. 2)

Since they were first issued, the uses of the RDAs have expanded to multiple purposes that could not have been envisioned by the committee that created them. The 10th edition (NRC, 1989), the version in current use, states that

> [F]rom their original application as a guide for advising "on nutrition problems in connection with national defense," the RDA's have come to serve other purposes: for planning and procuring food supplies for population subgroups; for interpreting food consumption records of individuals and populations; for establishing standards for food assistance programs; for evaluating the adequacy of food supplies in meeting national nutritional needs; for designing nutrition education programs; for developing new products in industry; and for establishing guidelines for nutrition labeling of foods. (p. 10)

THE RECOMMENDED DIETARY ALLOWANCES: SOME LIMITATIONS

From the beginning, it was apparent to the RDA Committee that a single set of numeric values in tabular form, even with some accompanying text, was inadequate. For that reason, early editions describe a "dietary pattern" and even provide a low-cost menu illustrating how to meet the RDAs. Later editions stress the importance of getting essential nutrients from a variety of foods rather than by supplementation or by extensive fortification of single foods (NRC, 1980). The eighth edition takes the discussion of the importance of food somewhat further, observing that the RDAs do not take into account unrecognized nutritional benefits of food or the psychological and social needs they may meet (NRC, 1974).

Criticism of the RDAs as a single measure of dietary quality has grown with the increased appreciation of the role of dietary factors in health promotion. A parallel set of recommendations, the Dietary Guidelines for Americans (U.S. Department of Agriculture, 1980) was first released more than 15 years ago to address the role of dietary patterns and nutrient intakes in chronic, degenerative diseases. These guidelines, which by law must be revised every 5 years, have gained prominence as nutritional concerns have shifted from nutrient deficiencies to chronic disease prevention. Parallel sets of recommendations are difficult for practitioners to integrate. They are even more difficult for individuals to implement. Over time, the concept that chronic disease prevention should be included in the development of allowances has gained increasing support.

Lack of data is a fundamental limitation of the RDAs. The need for judgment in the absence of unequivocal data has always fueled controversy, and criticism has intensified as science has become increasingly complex and the need for more judgment in the absence of clear evidence has grown.

In commenting on problems related to the publication of the 10th edition, Sushma Palmer (1990), director of the FNB staff at the time they were published wrote:

> The primary basis of controversy is the inadequacy of the data base for establishing RDAs ... Controversy also arises because the *RDAs are themselves estimates of nutrient allowances derived from data that are often incomplete and difficult to interpret* (italics added). Thus considerable judgment is needed in analyzing these data, estimating the distribution of nutrient requirements in the population, assigning safety margins to account for inter- and intra-individual variability and times of increased need, and extrapolating these data to estimate nutrient allowances for different subgroups in the population. (p. 13)

Lacking an understanding of the distribution of individual requirements for most nutrients, the RDA committees follow a four-step process in setting requirements. They (a) agree on the basis for determining nutrient status, (b) estimate average requirement and variability in a given population, (c) determine the allowance by increasing the average requirement enough to meet the needs of nearly all members of the population, and (d) for some nutrients, increase the allowance to account for inefficiency of use of the nutrient as consumed (FNB, 1994). Each of these steps is accompanied by limited information for at least some nutrients, and in those instances, scientific judgment must be substituted. That usually results in the addition of safety factors to ensure that most people are covered.

The inexact nature of the process of setting nutritional recommendations is illustrated further by the fact that different countries, using essentially the same data, vary widely in their recommendations (Trichopoulou & Vassilakou, 1990). This is related not only to differences in judgment but also to the conflict that arises when individual nations independently select criteria on which to develop their own standards (Helsing, 1990). With the globalization of the food supply, the problem of inconsistent standards, especially when their use is extended to food labeling, will become increasingly important. Indeed, harmonization of North American standards is an agenda item for the committee working on the next RDAs revision.

A growing body of information documents interactions among nutrients and among nutrients and drugs. This, along with the recently developed concept of bioavailability of nutrients and consideration of pharmacologic effects of several nutrients consumed in amounts far greater than those achievable through dietary means, further complicates the picture. All of these issues must be considered in revisions of the RDAs.

RDAS IN TRANSITION

The committee that produced the first RDAs surveyed the research literature and formulated a tentative set of nutrient values. It then circulated a draft among the community of 50 or so nutrition scientists with relevant research interests to get their reactions (Roberts, 1958). Recent estimates have put the current number of nutrition scientists as high as 20,000 (Marriott, Wotecki, & Greenwood, 1994), making the democratic process, critical to acceptance of the standards, ever more unwieldy.

The first edition specified allowances for calories and 8 nutrients: protein, calcium, vitamin A, thiamin, riboflavin, niacin, and ascorbic acid. In contrast, the 10th edition includes recommendations for calories and 19 nutrients and a supplementary table where data are considered sufficient only to recommend estimated "safe and adequate daily dietary intakes" for 7 others (NRC, 1989, p. 6).

It is interesting to observe just how limited the evidence was at the time the first RDAs were published. The text that explains how the RDA for each nutrient was established cites the work of one or two research laboratories that provided all of the data then available. It was a conservative document, that admitted frankly the weakness of the data in some areas. After the publication of the first document, the FNB continued to appoint a committee to prepare each new edition and anonymous reviewers read and critiqued each report. Recent committees have sought additional expertise through correspondence, workshops, and special meetings with invited experts (FNB, 1994).

In preparing newer editions, committees have examined six types of evidence: (a) nutrient intakes of apparently healthy people; (b) field studies in which clinical signs of nutrient deficiencies are corrected by dietary improvement; (c) balance studies that measure nutritional status in relation to intake; (d) nutrient depletion–repletion studies in which participants are maintained on diets containing marginally low or deficient levels of a nutrient, followed by correction of the deficit, with measured amounts of the nutrient; (e) extrapolation from animal experiments; and (f) biochemical measurements that assess the degree of tissue saturation or adequacy of molecular function in relation to nutrient intake (FNB, 1994). The last of these types of evidence, the biochemical measurements, introduces a concept that early committees could not consider: The idea of nutrient levels not only to prevent deficiencies, but also to provide for optimal function.

THE 11TH EDITION: RDAS RECONCEPTUALIZED

After it disbanded, the deadlocked committee that was to prepare the 10th edition, the FNB prepared a statement that raised a series of critical questions. The report questioned the definition of the RDAs themselves:

> Does the definition of the RDAs apply only to the prevention of deficiency diseases or generally to the promotion of growth, maintenance of good health, and reduction of risk from other diseases? What are the physiological indicators of *good* health? Can *optimal* health be defined? (FNB, 1986, p. 483)

The report raised questions about every aspect of the process: The criteria used to establish the RDAs, the databases and methodologies used in the decision-making process, and the age and sex groupings used in the tables. Finally, the report asked whether the values applied to individuals or to groups. This last and very critical question has generated considerable debate on questions of statistically appropriate methodologies. When the 10th edition finally appeared, it was clear that controversy had risen to a level that demanded a redesign of the structure of the RDAs.

As the FNB approached the prospect of the 11th edition, members disagreed with each other about the status of the scientific database underlying the RDAs, the need to revise the report, and whether the traditional concept encompassed current knowledge about nutrition and health promotion throughout life (FNB, 1994). It was clear that the process would need drastic revision if a new document could ever be produced.

As a first step, in June 1993, the FNB held a symposium "Should the Recommended Dietary Allowances Be Revised?" A public hearing followed. The purpose was to provide an open forum to begin a dialogue with the community of scientists and RDA users to explore what they as consumers would want the RDAs to be. The FNB also participated in meetings sponsored by other relevant professional organizations. The deliberations concluded that (a) sufficient new knowledge has accumulated for selected nutrients that a review of the current RDAs is warranted, (b) reduction in the risk of chronic disease is a concept that should be included in the formulation of future RDAs where sufficient data for efficacy and safety exist, and (c) serious consideration must be given to developing a new format for future RDAs. These activities led to the production of a paper that outlines a conceptual approach for the next revision in which the RDAs will become part of a more comprehensive effort (FNB, 1994).

A new committee structure has now been established. It includes a Standing Committee on the Scientific Evaluation of Dietary Reference Intakes as well as a series of subcommittees. The task list is ambitious. Dietary Reference Intakes (DRIs) will be developed for each nutrient or nonnutrient food component for which adequate scientific data are available. They will include (a) estimated average requirements and standard deviation by age and sex, (b) recommended dietary allowances, based on the estimated average and deviation, and (c) maximum intake levels above which risk of toxicity would increase.

The DRIs will be based on scientific evidence concerning (a) intake from food and supplements, (b) bioavailability, (c) absorption, metabolism, and nutrient interaction, (d) the role of each nutrient in preventing or delaying the onset of chronic disease or developmental abnormalities, and (e) functional indicators demonstrating a causal relation between dietary components and chronic disease or developmental abnormalities.

Under the coordination of the standing committee, these efforts will lead to the publication of a series of reports. Responding to criticism of the lack of documentation for decisions in earlier editions, each volume will provide the rationale for each recommendation. It will include a literature review, a description of the methods used to make decisions, and recommendations for future research. Appropriate guidance for potential users of these documents will be incorporated into the final reports. The number of special needs categories for which values will be provided will increase from 13 to 19, covering such subjects as age, gender, and special needs categories (Nutrition Reviews, 1996).

For the first time, this effort goes beyond U.S. borders as a joint project with Health Canada. Mexico is also expected to participate. Whether the new approach will provide a more useful approach to nutritional assessment is already a matter of debate.

RDAS AND STANDARDS OF ACADEMIC ACHIEVEMENT: ARE THERE PARALLELS?

The value of looking critically at the RDAs for guidance in setting educational standards lies in the lessons of process, both the successes and the setbacks, and in an examination of their use. A review of more than five decades of history of the RDAs and of the important milestones in their development suggests several important and transferable ideas:

- In the case of dietary recommendations, it has been clear from the outset that no single standard can serve as an adequate yardstick against which to measure the concept of *nutritional well-being* even among relatively homogeneous populations. In the field of education, most would agree that the types of inferences one can draw about the performance of American youth are also limited by reliance on a single measure; different types of measurements to evaluate different components of academic achievement even within a single subject area are also necessary. Data about student performance on tasks that extend over time, that rely on group activity, and that cross disciplinary boundaries may well provide a more complete picture of student achievement than those based on a more conventional, discrete assessment. Data on teacher professional development, curriculum and instruction, and resources also may be telling.
- RDAs have always involved judgment. That alone guarantees that although it is often possible to achieve consensus, unanimity of opinion is unlikely. Judgment and controversy have been greatest in areas where data are most deficient. Early committees chose to set recommendations for nutrients for which the evidence was most convincing and to expand the basis for judgment as new data became available. The tensions surrounding the combination of insufficient data and human judgment also mark educational standard setting. Again, data used in standard setting for National Assessment of Educational Progress (NAEP) are incomplete; the data come from a single measure and are influenced in unknown ways both by students' motivation to perform well on a low-stakes assessment and by limited information about the teaching and learning opportunities that precede the assessment. Raters' (perhaps differing) values about the levels at which high academic achievement should be manifest also influence the standards. This iterative process used in successive revisions of the RDAs may serve as a model for setting standards in education.
- In the case of the RDAs, the table of values that summarizes nutrient recommendation, gives an unjustified illusion of precision. Many of the problems associated with the interpretation of the RDAs have arisen because of such fundamental and critical problems as failure to go beyond the tables to read and understand the explanatory text (Beaton, 1985). In setting any standards, serious effort should be devoted to adequate documentation of the decisions that underlie

them and to educational efforts to help users of these standards to interpret them correctly. Indeed, the plan for the next revision of the RDAs includes the production of a specific user's guide to facilitate the process. The provision of contextual and explanatory information in education standard setting also is critical to the intelligent use of findings by policy makers and others.

- Similarly, in both nutrition and education, the pressure for broad, and in some cases unintended, use of the standards is evident. Over time in both contexts, users (and even sponsors of the standard-setting efforts) have expanded the objectives to be served by the standards. In both fields, stakeholders use standards as a yardstick against which to measure progress, as a lever for promoting change and communicating performance goals, as an evaluative tool, and as a referent for international performance. In nutrition, like education, one can question whether the standards can serve multiple and varied purposes simultaneously and equally well.
- Reconceptualizing the evaluation framework for the increasingly complex structure of *optimal nutrition* has been difficult and not without its critics. Yet, it attempts to respond to the demands of newer knowledge. It is reasonable to suggest that the measurement of educational achievement will experience similar growing pains as it refines its conception of education achievement and seeks more inclusive and relevant measures of achievement.
- Finally, the lessons of setting RDAs underscores the importance of providing opportunities for discussion of alternative views. The members of the first RDA committee recognized that acceptance of the RDAs depended on an inclusive and democratic process that provided a forum for discussion and serious consideration of alternative viewpoints (Roberts, 1958). Those responsible for the next revision, facing far greater controversies than ever before, have returned to this very open approach as a critical step toward producing a document that will be accepted and used. The NAEP program recognizes this important need and seeks broad input on the products of standard setting.

If one approaches the establishment of guidelines as both a science and an art, it is reasonable to consider that there are parallel and creative approaches for both disciplines. There are also parallel overriding questions that both communities should ask:

1. Are there ways to better combine empirical data and judgment in standard setting?
2. How can the uncertainties and complexities of the field be reduced to meaningful indicators without compromising scientific validity?
3. Are there ways to streamline the "unwieldy democratic process" in the setting and implementing of standards?
4. When statistical analyses are used, what methods would be most fitting and appropriate?

5. How can the information be effectively reported for multiple audiences and users?

REFERENCES

Beaton, G. H. (1985). Uses and limits of the recommended dietary allowances for evaluating dietary intake data. *American Journal of Clinical Nutrition, 1,* 155–164.

Food and Nutrition Board. (1943). *Recommended dietary allowances* (Series No. 115). Washington, DC: National Research Council.

Food and Nutrition Board. (1948). *Recommended dietary allowances, revised 1948* (Series No. 129). Washington, DC: National Research Council.

Food and Nutrition Board. (1986). Recommended dietary allowances: Scientific issues and process for the future. *Journal of Nutrition, 116,* 482–488.

Food and Nutrition Board. (1994). How should the recommended dietary allowances be revised? *Nutrition Reviews, 52,* 216–219.

Helsing, E. (1990). Problems in the process of formulating an RDI. *European Journal of Clinical Nutrition, 44*(2), 33–36.

Marriott, B. M., Wotecki, C., & Greenwood, M. R. C. (1994). Should the RDAs for the United States be revised? *Biblioteca Nutritio Dietetica, 51,* 180–182.

National Research Council. (1974). *Recommended dietary allowances* (8th Rev. ed.). Washington, DC: National Academy Press.

National Research Council. (1980). *Recommended dietary allowances* (9th Rev. ed.). Washington, DC: National Academy Press.

National Research Council. (1989). *Recommended dietary allowances* (10th Rev. ed.). Washington, DC: National Academy Press.

Nutrition Reviews. (1996). Revisiting dietary allowances and requirements. *Nutrition Reviews, 54,* 246–247.

Palmer, S. (1990) Recommended dietary allowances (10th ed.). *European Journal of Clinical Nutrition, 44*(2), 13–21.

Roberts, L. J. (1958). Beginnings of the recommended dietary allowances. *Journal of the American Dietetic Association, 34,* 903–908.

Trichopoulou, A., & Vassilakou, T. (1990). Recommended dietary intakes in the European community member states: An overview. *European Journal of Clinical Nutrition, 44*(2), 51–126.

U.S. Department of Agriculture. (1980). Nutrition and your health: Dietary guidelines for Americans. *Home and Garden Bulletin, 232.*

Science and Judgment in Environmental Standard Setting

Sheila Jasanoff
Department of Science and Technology Studies
Cornell University

Environmental regulation, like educational policy, crucially depends on the establishment and enforcement of standards. One can observe numerous similarities in the interplay of social, political, and technical issues in educational and environmental standard setting. In this article, I review several major types of environmental standards (design, performance, exposure, safety, and behavioral) and discuss their points of contact with educational standards. In this article, I highlight areas of judgment common to both standard-setting processes and describe the principal mechanisms that are used to improve the credibility of environmental standards. In conclusion, I suggest ways in which experiences gained in the environmental arena could usefully be extended to the educational arena.

Modern environmental regulation shares with educational policy a basic commitment to establishing and enforcing standards. For those involved in educational standard setting, as in the National and State Assessments of Educational Progress (NAEP), a closer look at environmental standards may provide new analytic tools and conceptual clarification. Bland and bureaucratic on the surface, standard setting is actually a deeply value-laden process that calls for special skills, expert judgment, and continual exercise of discretion (Jasanoff, 1990; Salter, 1988). In this article, I describe the principal types of standards used in the field of environmental protection and the judgments involved in their development and implementation. Mechanisms that constrain expert judgment are discussed, as well as the relevance of particular aspects of environmental standard setting to NAEP.

To understand the complexities of environmental standard setting and to tease apart their implications for education, it is useful to begin with an ambiguity latent

---

Requests for reprints should be sent to Sheila Jasanoff, Department of Science and Technology Studies, Cornell University, 632 Clark Hall, Ithaca, NY 14853–2501.

in the meaning of the term *standard*. A standard, on one hand, is a measure of high performance that all should strive to achieve. It is "a degree or level of requirement, excellence, or attainment" (as defined in the *American Heritage Dictionary,* 1969, p. 1256). In the environmental context, standards are often required by law to protect the most vulnerable populations or to ensure reasonable levels of safety, health, and environmental quality for those most at risk. At the same time, a standard is a powerful averaging instrument that requires conformity from everyone it affects. It is in this sense "an acknowledged measure of comparison for quantitative or qualitative value; criterion; norm" (*American Heritage Dictionary,* 1969, p. 1256). Thus, environmental standards demand a stated minimum level of performance from entire industries and product classes, regardless of the specific needs, circumstances, or characteristics of individual members.

Standards designed to set a floor for performance could, in the environmental as in the educational arena, imperceptibly end up defining the ceiling as well, unless law or policy explicitly provides otherwise. The so-called nondegradation policy under the U.S. Clean Air Act, for example, specified that regions with cleaner than mandated air quality could not allow pollution levels to rise to the extent permitted by the standards. Despite some such provisions for regional variation, vehement scientific and political controversies have arisen around environmental standards because of the need to impose uniform criterion of good performance across an extraordinary diversity of situations and actors.

In environmental as in educational policy, demonstrating that standards actually work involves complex challenges. The purpose of any environmental standard is to keep some preconceived type of harm from occurring. Failure to comply may produce visibly adverse results, as at the Three Mile Island nuclear plant in Pennsylvania or in the polluted Los Angeles air basin. For many environmental standards, however, it is impossible to demonstrate, in real time, whether their purpose is actually being met. This could be because the beneficial effects of the standard are too small to measure against background noise, too far off in time to be detected by current monitoring, or attributable to factors other than the implementation of the standard. The credibility of environmental standards accordingly depends more often on the methods by which they were generated and enforced than on their validation against observable natural phenomena.

TYPES OF ENVIRONMENTAL STANDARDS

Environmental standards come in many forms and from many sources. They may apply to industrial processes, pollutants, facilities, products, equipment, vehicles, or natural media, such as air and water. Standards may be used to (a) regulate the quality of an environmental medium; (b) control harmful discharges, emissions, and residues; (c) establish limits for human exposure to toxic substances; (d) specify

ENVIRONMENTAL STANDARDS 109

safe usage conditions for regulated products; or (e) influence environmentally detrimental behaviors. They may be required by law (regulatory standards), recommended by guidelines, or voluntarily adopted by industries or private standard-setting organizations (consensus standards). They may be enforced through rigorous monitoring and sanctions or through relatively lax systems of self-regulation. Whatever their origin or specific context of application, environmental standards can be classified into several major types, as described below.

Design Standards

Regulatory programs sometimes specify design characteristics that must be complied with to satisfy environmental requirements. Such *design standards* are generally regarded as the most rigid form of regulatory standard, but they have the offsetting virtue of being relatively unambiguous and hence easy to monitor and enforce. They resemble in this respect such educational standards as the need to complete a minimum number of courses for a high school diploma. As with comparable standards for education, questions often arise about the fit between environmental design standards and the outcomes they seek to achieve.

The most common design standards are those that govern the engineering of technological artifacts or systems. Thus, the U.S. Environmental Protection Agency (EPA) has stipulated under its clean air program that cars should be fitted with catalytic converters, that utility companies should install scrubbers or tall smokestacks, or that designated monitoring equipment should be used to check motor-vehicle emissions. Equally significant in impact are design standards that control the production and validation of scientific information used as a basis for environmental regulation. For example, under the Toxic Substances Control Act, EPA has prescribed the tests that chemical manufacturers must conduct to establish product safety. More generally, detailed federal protocols govern the conduct of bioassays or clinical trials, good laboratory practices, informed consent of human participants, and animal welfare. Studies failing to meet these standards may not be admitted as evidence in the regulatory process. Similarly, federal risk assessment guidelines prescribe the methods that regulators and industry must follow in estimating the risk to humans from a mixed bag of evidence, including epidemiological studies, rodent or other animal studies, and in vitro studies. Such standards are perpetually open to challenge for failure to keep up with changes in scientific knowledge.

Performance Standards

Whereas design standards target the components of a technological system, *performance standards* seek to regulate the quality of its output—in other words, to specify how the system as a whole should perform. They are most similar in intent to educational standards that stipulate how students should perform at different proficiency levels. Thus, a performance standard for the automobile industry may prescribe a level of fuel economy to be attained by each car (e.g., 27.5 miles per gallon) or maximum allowable concentrations for each pollutant emitted by its exhaust system. In contrast, design standards may seek to accomplish the same outcomes by specifying exactly what types of fuels, filters, pipes, and converters should be used by different vehicle types. Performance standards are prized by regulated industries for their relative flexibility because they leave to industrial managers the choice of how to achieve the desired level of performance and at what cost. Nonetheless, conflicts routinely occur not only about the levels at which the standard is set but also about the choice of performance parameter that the standard addresses (e.g., emissions reductions vs. reduced health risks, reductions in cancer mortality vs. reductions in ecological damage).

The boundary between a design standard and a performance standard is not entirely clear-cut. What looks like a performance standard for a technological subsystem may look suspiciously like a design standard for the larger system in which it is embedded. The level of organization at which performance standards should be pegged accordingly is a major conceptual issue for environmental regulators. Perhaps the best known example in recent years concerned the so-called bubble policy adopted by EPA to regulate discharges of air pollutants from large industrial facilities, such as steel mills or petrochemical plants. This policy allowed managers to treat the entire plant as if it were encased in a single imaginary bubble. Emissions leaving the bubble could then be aggregated and regulated as if from a single source, rather than regulating each smokestack or emission source under the bubble separately—and at potentially far greater cost. Extension of such a policy to education, so as to leave some school districts unremediated while raising overall averages, would pose potentially insurmountable ethical and political dilemmas.

Exposure Standards

Exposure is an important concept in educational as well as environmental standard setting—exposure to ideas and topics in the former, and to hazards in the latter. Many environmentally harmful substances are controlled by means of standards that limit human exposure. Thus, ambient air and water quality standards guard entire populations against excessive exposure. Standards governing pesticide residues on raw or processed foods, radiation levels in and around nuclear power plants, and the quality of drinking water constitute additional examples. *Exposure standards* are based on information about the structures and activities of chemicals, their toxicological properties, the levels and pathways of human exposure, and animal and epidemiological studies of their health effects. Techniques used in standard setting include both qualitative characterizations, typically based on the weight of the evidence, and quantitative risk assessment based on mathematical models.

Both educators and environmentalists confront the problem that there is no such thing as a "typical" exposure. As EPA's 1996 proposals to regulate ozone and airborne particulates made clear, a central question in establishing exposure standards is who should be protected: everyone (from the most to the least vulnerable), the "average" person, children, the sick, the elderly, the economically disadvantaged, those already subjected to exceptional risks, and so forth. In the environmental arena, this problem may be solved by law. For example, the U.S. Clean Air Act amendments of 1990 provided that standards for toxic air pollutants should aim to protect the *maximally exposed individual* (*MEI;* National Research Council [NRC], 1994). Critics of the act noted that such a policy would not necessarily advance public health because the maximally exposed individual was not necessarily the one most at risk.

Product Safety Standards

More important for the environment than for education, this extremely common type of standard specifies characteristics that certain regulated product classes must meet to obtain marketing approval. Pesticide formulations, for example, may be required to contain no more than prescribed levels or combinations of active ingredients. Wastes to be deposited in ordinary landfills may be banned from including substances listed as "hazardous." Limits may be placed on the heavy metal content of sewage sludge processed for application to agricultural lands. Construction equipment may have to be designed so as to meet noise control standards. As in the case of exposure standards, *product safety standards* are based on data about exposure levels, effects, and pathways. They are generally enforced through product licensing or registration. They resemble in these respects standards for textbook content in education.

Standards of Practice and Behavior

Standards regulating environmentally harmful products and processes are often supplemented by requirements that control how people should handle or manage them. This class of standards covers an immensely varied array of activities, including, most important, reporting requirements. Thus, federal law provides for "cradle to grave" regulation of waste management, specifying safety requirements for each step in the production, transport, disposal or reuse of such materials. Property owners on whose land an endangered species has been found or who own a designated wetland are required by law to undertake various protective measures. Manufacturers of toxic substances are legally bound to carry out enough tests to permit meaningful risk assessment of their products. Builders of large, federally regulated facilities (dams, highways, power plants) are required to perform environmental impact assessments in accordance with prescribed standards. In each context, behavioral prescriptions are based on relevant information about safety, health, or environmental sustainability. *Behavioral standards* are likely to raise below-par performance, as also in the educational arena, but they may deter innovation.

JUDGMENT CALLS

Environmental standards, like educational standards, attempt to impose a degree of uniformity on complex systems that, in the case of the environment, comprise such heterogeneous elements as natural resources, scientific information, technological artifacts, and human behavior. The primary goal of standards is to protect human beings and the environment against harms that can be reasonably foreseen. Environmental standards accordingly are generally based on predictive exercises, such as risk assessments, that are carried out on the basis of imperfect knowledge. Data gaps are endemic in environmental (and educational) standard setting, and confusion often exists about the causes, boundaries, duration, and extent of the problem that the standard seeks to control. The available information tends to support divergent assessments of risk, and because environmental standards can have far-reaching economic and social consequences, the interpretation of data becomes highly political. The judgments that scientists and regulators make in the course of establishing standards reflect these limitations. These judgments can be grouped as follows.

Boundaries of (Regulatory) Science

Environmental standards almost always involve a component of scientific or technical assessment that entails more judgment than may be apparent to the casual observer. For decades, controversy about standards has centered on the demand that regulators should use "good science" as a basis for their standardizing decisions. Yet, contrary to the intuition of many participants in the regulatory process, what counts as science (let alone as good science) for policy purposes is frequently contested. The boundaries of science have to be periodically renegotiated and redefined in the course of standard setting; where to draw the line between science on the one hand and policy on the other is a recurrent issue (Jasanoff, 1990). Standard-setting organizations function most effectively when they recognize and allow for appropriate boundary revisions to take place as knowledge changes and social preferences evolve.

Principles for assessing the risks of potentially carcinogenic chemicals supply one well-known example. Although many today speak of cancer risk assessment as a science (albeit sometimes as a *young, immature,* or *infant* science), as little as 20 years ago most practitioners and observers viewed this same process as policy. What happened in the intervening period? Changes in scientific knowledge and its social context permitted stronger claims to be made on behalf of the scientific status of risk assessment.

First, some parts of the risk assessment process indeed became more scientific in a conventional sense. Thus, more basic biological knowledge accumulated about the mechanisms by which cancer is initiated and promoted, about the pharmacokinetics of particular chemicals, and about interspecies differences in susceptibility to different forms of cancer. These and related findings were gradually incorporated into risk assessment. Second, the performance of risk assessment became more professional and systematic, with strong institutional bases developing in universities, consulting firms, and professional societies as well as in regulatory agencies. Third, with greater professionalism, it became possible to subject risk assessments to peer review and even to limited replication, thereby enhancing the claim of objectivity. The NRC (1983) provided powerful support for the idea that risk assessment is a science with a report that called for strict separation between risk assessment and risk management; policy and value judgments were largely seen as influencing the latter process but not the former.

At bottom, however, cancer risk assessment still rests on choices that can only be regarded as policy-driven. Chief among these is the decision to accept data generated in animal studies as a surrogate for direct observation of adverse effects in humans, a decision that entails additional elements of choice. For example, although several mathematical models have been developed for extrapolating risk estimates from animals to humans, this exercise incorporates value judgments that have been widely discussed in the literature (e.g., see Graham, Green, & Roberts, 1988; NRC, 1994). The shape of the dose-response curve at very low levels of exposure is still a matter for speculation, guesswork, and precautionary policy. In particular, the standard assumption of linearity at low doses (as opposed to, say, a hockey-stick shape) yields relatively high-risk estimates, and hence is preferred by regulators wishing to (or legally compelled to) err on the side of safety.

In sum, although cancer risk assessment is now seen as falling on the science side of the science-policy boundary, it continues to incorporate elements that look very much like policy. The objectivity of risk assessment is maintained in part through social and institutional arrangements, such as peer review and expert advice, that have been developed to separate science from politics. Comparable problems of ensuring objectivity and reliability may also arise in the establishment of educational standards.

Equivalence and Simplification

The comparison and establishment of equivalences are integral to all forms of standard setting. A standard, to begin with, is itself a unit of comparison. It is the norm against which every instance of the product, process, or system governed by the standard has to be measured. Adopting a standard, moreover, implies that equivalence has been established within the class of objects to which the standard applies. It would be pointless to set a standard for a thing that is unique, such as a work of art. Only when the regulated universe contains multiple or recurrent instances of the same kind of thing—things that are by definition comparable—does it make sense to control them by means of a standard. Finally, in the process of standard setting it is often necessary to assume equivalence between a model or an artificial test system that is used to produce data and the real-world system that is to be regulated. Each of these equivalence determinations requires the exercise of judgment and can be highly political.

The problem of equivalence forcefully presents itself to both educational and environmental policymakers because their standards are devised to protect entire populations. Of concern to environmentalists, individuals within a given population may be highly variable in their susceptibility to any particular source of harm. Some may be genetically predisposed to illness. Others may be specially vulnerable because of their age, sex, lifestyle, or overall state of health. Some people may have habits, such as smoking or eating fatty foods, that increase their risk above that of other similarly situated people. To set standards that protect a reasonable cross-section of the population, regulatory agencies have to decide how much of this variability they will factor into their decisions and in what manner. Criteria for when to presume uniformity and when to allow for variance are usually lacking. A typical choice is to simplify variability by assuming the existence of a standard (but, by the same token, mythical) person: one who consumes a specified number of calories from designated food categories, drinks a constant volume of water, takes a fixed amount of exercise, and spends unvarying amounts of time each day at work, at home, or on the road. The concept of the MEI under the U.S. Clean Air Act is just one example, in this case legislatively decreed, of such a standardized person.

Simplification is also unavoidable when standards are based on models or other surrogate data sources. In the example of cancer risk assessment previously noted, animals have to be considered sufficiently like human beings to justify the use of bioassays in estimating risk to people. For this equivalence to hold, many points of divergence between humans and animals have to be presumed irrelevant (e.g., body weight, metabolism, diet, life span). Variations between reality and models must similarly be overlooked when properties of ecosystems are examined through laboratory-based experimental systems, field studies, or computer simulations. As knowledge evolves, models may be made more complex to accommodate new findings, but this is a slow and costly process.

Controversies over regulatory standards frequently signal a breakdown in the credibility of the simplifications and equivalence judgments made by the responsible agency. In the widely publicized dispute over Alar, a plant growth regulator and potential carcinogen, the Natural Resources Defense Council (NRDC) successfully argued that EPA had failed to consider a relevant dimension of variability between adults and children in its standard-setting process. Children, NRDC claimed, were more at risk than adults from Alar because they had a lower average body weight and yet ate proportionally higher quantities of apple products (Jasanoff, 1990). Similarly, in disputes over air quality standards, industry representatives faulted EPA for presuming that the standard MEI would spend 70 years entirely outdoors, on a porch, downwind from a facility emitting toxic air pollutants. Dismissing the "porch potato" as completely unrealistic, EPA's critics and scientific advisers called for a model that was truer to known patterns of human behavior; by the mid-1990s, EPA had begun to replace MEI estimate with estimates of high-end and upper-bound exposures (NRC, 1994). The charge that EPA's cancer risk assessment principles are too conservative reflects similar questioning of the presumed equivalence between a model used in standard setting and the real world. For educators, comparable controversies are most likely to arise around policies designed (or not designed) for exceptional groups (e.g., children with disabilities or the specially gifted and talented).

Embedded Social Judgments

Although environmental standards generally aim to regulate physical processes and characteristics, they are frequently based on assumptions about the social world in which they will be implemented. In this way, standards that appear to be based exclusively on facts about nature and technology turn out also to incorporate assumptions about society. I use the term *embedded social judgment* to refer to these often unexamined and inexplicit assumptions about the behavior of human individuals, groups, and institutions. Such judgments are unavoidable in any system of standard setting, whether technical or social.

Safety standards for environmentally harmful products almost invariably contain embedded social judgments. For instance, a pesticide that is deemed to be "safe" will actually be so only under specified conditions of use that are presumed to prevail wherever the substance is marketed. Typically, pesticides should only be used at prescribed concentrations and applied only by properly trained people wearing appropriate protective clothing. Yet studies of farmworkers in the United States and abroad have shown that these practices are anything but uniform. Many pesticide applicators do not adequately protect themselves because they cannot afford the proper clothing. When pesticides are exported, use restrictions are not always followed because workers in the receiving country have not been adequately instructed about the risks of noncompliance. State enforcement authorities, chronically strapped for resources even in rich countries, do not carry out enough inspections to ensure that required health and safety practices are observed in the field.

Embedded social judgments can prove to be unwarranted even when problems of cross-cultural exchange and communication are not at issue. A recent striking example concerns the failed attempt by British regulatory authorities to stop the spread of bovine spongiform encephalopathy (BSE) in their country's cattle herds. The initial outbreak of the disease in 1986 led to a recommendation that BSE-contaminated meat and bone meal, the suspected transmission agent for BSE, no longer be fed to cattle. British officials apparently believed that the feed industry would instantly comply and that infectivity would drop to zero in due course. These assumptions turned out in retrospect to have been overly optimistic, in part, because they misconceived industry's willingness and ability to comply with the prescribed standard. Regulators had overlooked the fact that the same plants would continue to make the feed for pigs and chickens. Failure to clean out the equipment properly between processes may have resulted in cross-contamination of cattle feed. In addition, some farmers may have continued to use old, contaminated feed even after the ban went into effect. Finally, relatively low levels of compensation may have led to underreporting of BSE cases and to further risk of transmission. A narrow focus on the offending feed as the sole cause of the problem prevented a wider assessment of the social context within which the regulatory standard would have to be implemented.

Educational standards are similarly based on assumptions about the social world. In the case of NAEP, these include the assumption that school districts, teachers, and students will take the assessments seriously and will modify their behavior accordingly. This assumption, in turn, depends on acceptance of the view that NAEP results accurately measure educational achievement. Problems with any of these assumptions will undermine the efficacy of assessments.

Adequacy of Evidence

A fourth major kind of judgment that must be made in educational as well as environmental standard setting concerns the adequacy of the evidence on which standards are based. As previously noted, the production of evidence relevant to environmental standard setting is itself governed by a complex constellation of standards. Animal and epidemiological studies must conform to well-defined protocols. Quantitative risk assessments must be carried out in accordance with approved mathematical models. Field studies and laboratory experiments likewise must follow prescribed methods, and their results must generally be recorded and stored pursuant to formally approved "good laboratory practices."

Despite all of this attempted standardization, however, judgment is often called for in assessing the adequacy of scientific and technical evidence. As scientific knowledge changes, regulators have to determine whether earlier assumptions and analytic methods need to be revised or reevaluated. When, for example, is it appropriate to abandon a model in favor of data collected from actual observation of an environmental system? Under what conditions should a presumption of equivalence (e.g., that metabolic pathways are the same in mice and humans) be set aside on the basis of countervailing evidence? How, more generally, should regulators judge whether new scientific methods, including modeling approaches, are reliable enough to be used as a basis for costly decisions about public health and safety? Should exceptions from existing approaches to risk assessment continue to be made case by case, or has scientific knowledge progressed to the point of requiring an overhaul of the entire system?

As a legal matter, there is little question that environmental agencies have the discretion to answer such questions through any process that meets basic standards of administrative notice and comment (Jasanoff, 1995). Since its 1983 decision *Baltimore Gas & Electric Co. v. NRDC*, the U.S. Supreme Court has recognized that regulatory agencies are entitled to great deference from the courts when they make discretionary choices at the frontiers of science. Both earlier and later judicial decisions reviewing the adequacy of environmental standards also confirmed the view that agencies are not required to abide by scientific standards of proof when regulating to protect public health and safety. Nevertheless, courts can still overturn agency judgments with respect to environmental standards if they conclude that the scientific record does not support them or if the agency has not satisfactorily explained how it reached its decision.

Decisions to change existing analytic approaches on the basis of new data are always intensely political even when they meet applicable legal requirements. Any change in analytic methods is likely to bring about a change in standards, making them more or less stringent (Stern, 1991). In either case, settled expectations are likely to be disturbed and a political outcry may result. The primary mechanism that regulatory agencies have adopted to ensure the scientific and political credibility of such moves is consultation with expert advisory bodies. Evaluating the agency's assessment practices in the light of current science is a cardinal function of EPA's Science Advisory Board (SAB), a standing body with agency-wide jurisdiction, and its numerous subcommittees. EPA also appoints a variety of ad hoc committees to provide advice or peer review on specific issues as needed; such actions are sometimes undertaken in response to political pressure and sometimes under legislative mandate. Although these advisory bodies are selected for scientific and professional competence, it is widely recognized that their own legitimacy depends on their meeting basic criteria of diversity and representation, encompassing, for example, disciplines, gender, race, and geographical distribution.

EPA's change of course in assessing the risks of dioxin, once classified as the most potent human-made carcinogen, provides a striking example of the use of expert panels to ratify a new analytic approach. EPA had carried out its first dioxin risk assessment in 1985 largely on the basis of observed cancer incidence in animal studies. By 1988, when the agency revised its risk assessment, there were indications that dioxin may cause cancer by a specific molecular pathway—binding to an intracellular protein receptor—and that a new risk assessment model may be appropriate to take account of this mechanism (Johnson, 1995). The new model promised to lower dioxin's projected risks to human health, thereby prompting suspicion that EPA was bowing to industry pressure. Given the political saliency of dioxin, EPA correctly perceived that any reassessment of its risks would have to be supported by independent scientific advice. Key steps in gaining such legitimation were taken in 1988, when the SAB reviewed EPA's revised risk assessment and recommended that a new model be developed, and in 1990, when an expert meeting at Cold Spring Harbor, New York, concluded that the receptor-binding model was scientifically valid.

A more comprehensive review of EPA's risk-assessment practices was required by the 1990 Clean Air Act amendments. In view of the agency's increasing reliance on quantitative risk assessment to set air pollution standards, Congress asked EPA to seek advice from the NRC on how to improve its existing data collection and risk assessment practices and how to ensure that these practices would stay abreast of new developments in science. In the resulting report (NRC, 1994), an NRC committee concluded that EPA's basic approach of using conservative default assumptions in risk assessment was still reasonable, although the committee recommended the development of more explicit guidelines and standards to justify departures from these assumptions. The relative centralization of environmental policy in the federal government as well as its greater dependence on science, may make such processes of review and relegitimation more feasible for environmental than educational standard setting.

IMPLICATIONS FOR NAEP

A quarter century of governmental experience in environmental standard setting holds useful lessons for other areas in which standards play an important social role, as in the measurement of educational achievement under NAEP. Although the technicalities of environmental standard setting (e.g., the use of quantitative risk assessment) are not replicated in the educational context, generic issues relating to the credible exercise of judgment, the separation of scientific from policy concerns, and the legitimation of standards against a backdrop of knowledge change are common to both educational and environmental standard setting. The following points are particularly worth noting.

First, standards are invariably based on assumptions that reduce the complexity of the activity or system they regulate. Such simplifications may be accepted for long periods of time, but they may become contentious and eventually have to be abandoned if they are seen to contradict scientific consensus, common sense, or widespread political expectations. Regular review and critical monitoring of standards against validated data may keep embarrassing gaps from developing between the world as imagined by the standard-setting process and the world as perceived by the people most affected by the standard.

Second, even when standards are thought to be entirely scientific or technical (as in the environmental arena), they almost certainly contain embedded social judgments. Recognizing where assumptions are being made about social behavior and institutions—particularly, assumptions about the likely response to standards—is crucial to effective implementation. Unwarranted assumptions pose a risk to the legitimation of standard setting. To guard against tunnel vision or intellectual sloppiness, it is highly desirable for standard-setting processes to build in a capacity for institutional self-monitoring and self-criticism.

Third, various forms of boundary drawing are essential for the effective operation of any standard-setting procedure. In environmental standard setting, for example, it has proved important over time to maintain at least the appearance of a clear separation between judgments that are mainly scientific and judgments that are primarily political. Similar needs may well arise with respect to educational standard setting, where mechanisms for collecting information are more varied and less standardized. On the whole, standard-setting processes are most successful if they do not assume from the outset where the boundaries between objective knowledge and subjective policy should be drawn, but rely instead on structured negotiation to make such determinations in specific contexts.

Fourth, even with effective mechanisms for boundary drawing in place, standard-setting processes cannot avoid making value-laden choices that may have enormous social and political consequences. Tightening or relaxing standards invariably incurs charges of politicization. In the environmental context, agencies have achieved legitimacy for such choices through the strategic use of independent science, as represented in advisory committees that stand apart from the political process. Such institutional supports may prove important in the context of educational achievement standards as well, although here, even more than in connection with environmental standards, attention must be paid to the representativeness and social authority of bodies that offer technical advice.

ACKNOWLEDGMENTS

This article was commissioned by the Committee on the Evaluation of National and State Assessments of Educational Progress. The views expressed here are solely *my own.*

REFERENCES

American heritage dictionary. (1969). Boston: Houghton Mifflin.
Baltimore Gas and Electric Co. v. NRDC, 462 U.S. 87 (1983).
Graham, J. D., Green, L. C., & Roberts, M. J. (1988). *In search of safety: Chemicals and cancer risk.* Cambridge, MA: Harvard University Press.
Jasanoff, S. (1990). *The fifth branch: Science advisers as policymakers.* Cambridge, MA: Harvard University Press.
Jasanoff, S. (1995). *Science at the bar: Law, science and technology in America.* Cambridge, MA: Harvard University Press.
Johnson, J. (1995). Dioxin risk: Are we sure yet? *Environmental Science and Technology, 29,* 24A–25A.
National Research Council. (1983). *Risk assessment in the federal government: Managing the process.* Washington, DC: National Academy Press.
National Research Council. (1994). *Science and judgment in risk assessment.* Washington, DC: National Academy Press.
Salter, L. (1988). *Mandated science: Science and scientists in the making of standards.* Dordrecht, The Netherlands: Kluwer.
Stern, P. C. (1991). Learning through conflict: A realistic strategy for risk communication. *Policy Sciences, 24,* 99–119.

For Product Safety Concerns and Information please contact our EU
representative GPSR@taylorandfrancis.com
Taylor & Francis Verlag GmbH, Kaufingerstraße 24, 80331 München, Germany

www.ingramcontent.com/pod-product-compliance
Lightning Source LLC
Chambersburg PA
CBHW061419300426
44114CB00015B/1989